FURTHER THRIFTY FISHING

The Author on the Moored Jetty

FURTHER THRIFTY FISHING

By

N. K. ROBERTSON

(Author of *Thrifty Salmon Fishing*)

Illustrated by
OLIVIA ROBERTSON, MANNING ROBERTSON
and
L. A. ROBERTSON

HERBERT JENKINS LIMITED
3 DUKE OF YORK STREET
ST. JAMES'S LONDON S.W.1

First printing

Printed in Great Britain by Wyman & Sons Ltd., London, Reading and Fakenham

DEDICATED

TO
ARTHUR HUTTON
In appreciation of his encouragement

ACKNOWLEDGMENTS

To the proprietors of *The Field, Angling, Irish Angling, Salmon and Trout Magazine* for some of the material and illustrations re-used. I am indebted to Manning, Olivia, and L. A. Robertson for drawings and diagrams, and for the details supplied in the map, of which the outline was lent by the Irish Tourist Association. I have to thank the Irish Tourist Association and other friends for the use of photographs.

CONTENTS

LIST OF ILLUSTRATIONS

FURTHER THRIFTY FISHING

CHAPTER I

OUR ORIGINS AND SPECIES

(1) *Our Origins*

TAKING thrift as the common-sense way of making the most of what we might get, let us in this book consider why our sport is getting scarcer, and whether we can do better in preserving and sharing what is left. History confirms that civilization only increases the zeal of the votaries, for, as Thoreau puts it, " The pursuits of simple nations are the sports of the more artificial." It is likely that even more people with less cash will be seeking fewer fish. Why should we assume this ?

Archæology, history, literature and art combine to show that in time and space no other pastime has so much absorbed so constant a minority of malekind. This minority oppressed but never depressed, is entirely self-supporting. In 1944 the newsreels featured as history a row of old stalwarts on the Seine, holding their long bamboos, and barely turning their heads as the Relievers entered Paris. The same would have applied to any capital in Europe— except Dublin. Unlike the British Empire, which was won by Irishmen and sustained by women, the craft owes little to these two pervading forces. On the contrary, whilst the normal Irishman may be indifferent to fishing, the average women only tolerates the passion in the hope that by the indulgence her man may be distracted from some other one—worse.

Scholars have recorded the rich results of their researches

into angling origins, revealing the sequence from pure pot-hunting to the love of the game for itself ; both often co-existing. There is no surer index of refinement in civilization than the practice of angling as a form of leisure. Starting before recorded history, we will therefore try from the outset to distinguish between pot and pleasure. The pot probably began with the spear, and although the hook was eventually used as well, the net and the trap were better adapted to kill. The direct ancestor of the hook is believed to be the gorge used by cavemen, and acting on much the same principles as the keeper on a watch-chain—to jam in the fish's mouth. Examples of gorge bait-holders, of double-tapered bone suspended from the middle, are shown at La Madelaine and at Santa Cruz. Its successor, the hook, made of bone or thorn, instead of jamming, penetrated, " and which " (I quote from Plato) " from the nature of the operation is denoted Angling or drawing up." *Angle* itself is derived fom the ancient Aryan root, ANK = to bend, and upon it is suspended all that belongs to our art.

If not quite as old as the cave-men, bone hooks are as old as the females' counterpart, bone needles. To the anthropologist such angles are grouped under "Quest for Nourishment," and correctly so ; but good sportsmen admit that nourishment is not enough without the emotional urge. Our blood ancestors may have been concerned with pot-hunt, an honourable calling still pursued by the net-men of to-day, but our spiritual forebear was he who meticulously selected his curved bone, tickled its point with his thumb until—Hah ! the prick drew blood ! This precise and cherished angle of early man remains the factor upon which everything else has been and still is established. It involves what we cherish even if Plato decries : entice-ment—not attack ; timing, tremor, surprise, suspense, pace —until the captive bounces in beauty at our feet. This crudely simplified list of attractions may not satisfy the psychiatrist in his research for the emotional origins of the wide obsession derived from this shape of bone. He will discover neither combative nor amatory motives lurking in its marrow. No associative symbol has developed from it, such as the Hunter's Horn reflecting the guilty image of war ; nor the Bow and Arrow, typifying the stricken heart in love. I have never found the symbol of the hook in orthodox heraldry.

Leaving such analysis and pre-history, we take a familiar track and turn to the Greeks. As usual, they have left us an abundant legacy ; but we find that angling for pleasure was a very late development with them and merged into Roman times. The goddess Venus was traditionally associated with fish, perhaps more symbolically than with the angle. Being a sea people, they were disposed to scorn inland fish ; indeed, fish as a diet was not popular until later times and was chiefly consumed by the destitute. Homer allots no civic status to fishermen, yet he shows himself to be familiar with fishing devices, including the Rod. By the time of Herodotus fishermen rise in the social scale and metaphors, borrowed from the craft, are used in literature. Aristotle's interest was mainly scientific, as forming part of his *Natural History*, but this fishing experience was second-hand. Yet angling for the leisured must have existed when Plato (427–347 B.C.) addressed young men in part of a prayer for their welfare :*

" Fishing is not an occupation worthy of a man well born or well brought up, because it demands more of address and ruse than force, and is not for young people, like hunting, the occasion of healthy exercise."

Rebuffed by this aspersion of degeneracy, we are interested to find how much Theocritus (310–265 B.C.) stresses " the weary cares of men that live by toil " throughout the whole of his long and beautiful Idyll.†

* *The Laws*, VII, 823. Jowett's translation.
† *The Fisherman's Dream* (Idyll XXI, translated by A. Lang, 1889).

The same theme of hardship is voiced in the first Latin play.* Could two lines of dialogue be more dramatically terse and revealing ?

Q. " Shellfish gatherers, and hook-fishers, hungry race of men, how fare ye ? "
A. " Just as befits fishermen ; with hunger, thirst and expectation."

HUNGRY RACE OF MEN

Most of the Greek writers show sympathy and interest in the toilers, but it is not until the Romans, with the two Plinys, Ovid and, above all, Martial, that angling is fully recognized as a leisured sport. Pliny the Younger, perhaps eligible for what Plato had rebuked, remarks upon the agreeable situation of his villa from which " you may yourself fish, and lower your hook from your bedroom—almost from your very bed—just as from a little boat."

* " *Rudens*," by Plautus (*c.* 254–184 B.C.), Act II, Sc. 2.

Rome itself was on a river and inland influences were felt in Italy.

Martial's* lines of which the translation is now well defended by scholars :

> " Who has not seen the scarus rise,
>   Decoyed, and killed by fraudful flies ? "

must stir all our hearts. His less controversial

> *" Ecce redit sporta piscator inani "*

reflects not only sport, but the blank of a blank day. Martial further inspires our regard by his reputation of throwing back all mullets under three pounds weight.

Plutarch (c. A.D. 70) unjustifiably misquoted by Burton, in his *Anatomy*, was long regarded as antagonistic to the art. Actually his is the richest source of the lore and lure of his times. It was from him that Shakespeare derived his material for the world's most venerated joke when Cleopatra fooled Anthony. He tells of how Anthony, fearful of her known prowess with the angle, resolved to win the competition by hiring a diver to attach a fish to his hook. Cleopatra got wind of the plan and outwitted him by bribing the diver to use a salted fish. But it took Shakespeare himself to give these lines to Charmian and the Queen :

CHARMIAN :   I was merry when
> You wagered on your angling ; when your diver
> Did hang a salt fish on his hook, which he with
> fervency drew up."

CLEOPATRA :   " That time !—oh, times !—
> I laughed him out of patience, and that night
> I laughed him into patience ; and next morn,
> Ere the ninth hour, I drunk him to his bed."

Has ever sport inspired brighter gold ?
But of all Romans, Oppian, who wrote copiously about

* Ep., v. 18, 7 f.

it before he died at the age of thirty, was the absolute enthusiast of what he called " this lovely art." His specifica-
tion for a fisherman may make some of us uneasy.*

> ' First be the Fisher's limbs compact and sound,
> With solid flesh, and well braced sinews bound,
> Let due proportion every part commend,
> Nor leanness shrink too much, or fat distend."

Ælian (A.D. 170–230), a Roman, writing in Greek, has
given us the first known description of an artificial fly used
in Macedonia. He is not a writer with a great reputation
for accuracy, and to-day would probably be regarded more
as an efficient columnist ; but he has told us what no one
before him had mentioned, or no one following him for
another 1,400 years (until Dame Juliana), so we may
gratefully salute the tidings.

This is the historic dressing :

> " They fasten crimson red wool round a hook, and fix on to
> the wool two feathers which grow under a cock's wattles, and
> which in colour are like wax. Their rod is 6 feet long, and
> their line is the same length. Then they throw their snare,
> and the fish, attracted and maddened by the colour, come
> straight at it, thinking from the pretty sight to get a dainty
> mouthful ; when, however, it opens its jaws, it is caught by
> the hook and enjoys a bitter repast, a captive."—(Lambert's
> translation.)

We owe the re-discovery of this passage to Oliver, writing
in 1834. The charm of creating a " pretty sight " still
continues to beset fly dressers.

Because Ælian was the first to allude to this " new
method " is not to prove that experts on the Nile, or,
indeed, Martial himself, were not already familiar with
other " fraudful " lures. The Nile dominated Egypt, and

* Oppian III, 29, 31.

it is therefore appropriate that the first pictorial representation of fishing should be recorded there. The scene from Beni Hasan, c. 2,000 B.C., depicts a group of slaves (or gillies) angling, with rods and hand-lines, in delightfully realistic attitudes. We have to wait for 600 years until the Nile again gives us another picture, this time from Thebes, showing a bland, evidently distinguished gentleman patently fishing for " delight."

THE EGYPTIAN GENTLEMAN

Although Mesopotamia and Persia must have had constant communication with Egypt, there is no record of rod-fishing there ; neither is there in India, nor, still more strangely, in Israel. Neither the Old nor the New Testament allude to it. Inexplicable gaps such as these provide the unexplainable, which is the quality of both fish and fishermen.

To find mention of the rod in Asia one must go farther east—to China. According to Mr. Werner,* various contrivances for fishing occur during the B.C. millenium ;

* *Descriptive Sociology : Chinese,* by E. T. Werner.

while the use of silk for lines and of silkworm gut goes back
to pre-history. It was also an imperial pastime and a
philosophical exercise for sages. William Radcliffe,* at
whose quarry of learning those of us who are not equipped
for original research may fill our carts, tells of how one
Chiang Tzu-ya (of common extraction) rose to governance
in the empire (C. 1122 B.C.). He was an angler, but also
of a morally edifying habit. King Wen, the founder of
the Chou Dynasty, and one of the great sages—whence
perhaps his intelligent annexation of Chiang—for, as Mr.
Radcliffe says, all anglers *ex necessitate* are, or should be,
also sages—comes across our hero fishing with a piece of
straight iron instead of a barbed hook. This tackle, he
explains to the unrecognized monarch, is based on
voluntaryism, for only volunteers would suffer themselves
to be caught thuswise. Wen, from his many campaigns,
observed much and missed little. He noticed the full creel
lying at the sage's feet, and without more ado carried
Chiang off to his palace and installed him as Viceroy, term-
ing him my " Grand Father's Desire." The Chinese sage
is not only endowed with wisdom ; he has also worldly
wisdom, beside which one feels crude. After this tale one
is not astonished to learn that even the great Confucius
fished. " The master angled, but did not use a net." We
hear, too, as we might expect, of long and tapering bamboos, hooks of forged gold, variegated with silver or
green, and of lines decorated with feathers of the turquoise
kingfisher.

Both the Chinese and Japanese (a sea people with few
rivers) excelled in netting and trapping, and their exploits
furnish a motive for their designs in art.

In accounts of the later dynasties, where opulent Mandarins were more conspicuous than sages, one does not trace
the same disinterested exercise in the sport.

This telegraphic sketch of men holding hands down the
ages takes us to the Christian era, where the influence of

---

* *Fishing from the Earliest Times.* 1921. John Murray.

the Church is impressed on fishing history in England. Mr. Radcliffe has pointed out that even in the reign of Queen Elizabeth there were 145 days kept as fasts every year, and he suggests that the siting of eighteen bishoprics and two archbishoprics (out of twenty-seven Sees) on good salmon rivers can have been no coincidence. Even in these Christian days the connection with the Greek goddess was not forgotten, and Friday fish-day was still observed *dies veneris*.

It was the religious orders who introduced pike, carp and grayling to the Eastern Counties, from whence they gradually spread westward. In the reign of Edward I the novelty of pike made it twice as expensive to buy as the common salmon.

In England angling literature begins with the Book of St. Albans (1496), including Dame Juliana's *Treatyse* with her list of twelve artificial flies. I only wish that her authorship was, under higher criticism, not quite so apochryphal—but anyhow some lady of that name must have cared for fishing. We may pride ourselves that the subject of fishing should have been considered worthy to be printed among the very first few books in England.

The *Compleat Angler* (1656) overshadows every other book in the angler's library, " compleat," indeed, in lore and craft and fired with that humanity and comradeship dear to Englishmen. It is the common property of all who cast the angle for any type of fish in these islands, and in the waters of the English-speaking world. Now, since we realize that St. Peter did not handle a rod, we must leave him as patron to the net-men and establish Isaac as our special exemplar. After Shakespeare and Pepys, he is the Kalender Makers' standby for quotation.

A religion is justified by its saints, and a pastime by the character of its votaries. That so many men famed in public life, literature and art should for 4,000 years have found in angling an edifying distraction from mundane cares is proof of its honourable origin.

B

(2) *Our Species*

If our glance back teaches anything it would be how
little anglers have changed ; we are in temperament akin
to our forerunners. The old Egyptian gentleman could be
led from his arm-chair by the Nile and take his seat on the
Thames without noticing any difference. Indeed, until
recently competition experts on that river still preferred
the " tight " line attached to the top of their long rods
for range and for striking power. It was not until men
from Sheffield introduced the light, shorter rods with running
lines that the southerners were worsted and reluctantly
changed their form of attack.

One might be disposed to fancy that country men were
naturally keener fishers than town folks, yet experience
will confirm that those who are forced to dwell in cities
crave for escape and outdoor contemplation. Angling is
(as Plato implied) a refined, not a barbarous, sport. Ruse
is as essential to-day as it was when the Macedonian con-
trived his " pretty sight."

The materials furnishing the angler's simple outfit have,
of course, been extended by the use of tempered steel; by
the development from Indian grass (now known to have
been jute) and from horsehair to silken threads and filaments.
Such improvements, however, are an advance, but are not
revolutionary ; probably those lines used by Confucius were
as good or better than ours. The change is far less than
we can trace in any other sport. The older Mycenæan hooks
and those described by Plutarch have, it may be claimed,
a better bend—or ANK—than the Limerick hook. Compare our gradual advance with the evolution from bow and
arrow to gun and rifle ; or the immense differences of pace
in hunting, due to the specialized breeding of horses and
hounds ! Our plummet and the float are practically identical
with those used by earliest man. Even the split cane rod
is made from the same type of organic substance. Fashioned

by hand, it continues its—literally—bowing acquaintance with the reed cut from the waterside.

Nevertheless, left-hand influences have cast sinister and warning shadows, beginning where one should, I suppose, suspect revolution, in the reel. The art of living does not lie in being static, but in knowing where to halt. There can be no rule to guide us, saving that right judgment which enables a wise man to see ahead. Isaac Walton recognized that the wheel half-way up the rod, which intro-duced the running line, was a simple mechanical advance to be welcomed. Until then the man who hooked a big fellow could only throw his rod into the water and anxiously await eventualities : salmon fishing was an impossibility. With the running line, both fine and heavy fishing increased in interest and variety, while more opportunities were pre-sented for skill in hand and eye. The introduction of the ratchet reel, including the earlier Nottingham and Malloch types for spinning, could hardly have been opposed by the most conservative.

After those innovations, it is hard to say how far im-proved technical equipment has helped or menaced sport. There is no logical answer but, as any keeper will confirm, logic is the prerogative of lunatic asylums. We may, however, suggest that any device which vastly increases individual range during the present shortage of fishing water must become a nuisance. Even if we had unlimited elbow-room, it could still be argued that the more the angler delights in preserving independence of the mechanical product, the better will the spirit of the sport be preserved. It is not only a matter of skill. It takes a good technician to handle a complicated device, but it needs an artist to exploit the simple one. Compare the use of an expensive camera with the power of a fourpenny pencil ! Of all the dangers threatening our sport to-day, surely the worst would be to subordinate the hand to the cog-wheel, and to aspire to achieve the foolproof ? One unrestricted threadliner could ruin a beat of its stock of trout.

If we glance again at the companion sport of shooting, we see that the bow and arrow is still enjoyed as an accomplishment, but the blunderbuss that superseded it—hundreds of years later—hangs dusty on the wall. The naturally primitive (as distinct from the neo-archaic) will always hold its allure. Men will throw balls till the end of time, whilst mechanical equipment becomes antiquated and is scrapped, or it defeats its own ends. Only the very simple is sure to survive. Old sporting prints portray delightful compositions of a few shooters, dogs and beaters with a background of wood and field. In them men and nature form an enviable unity. To-day we pay high prices to possess *bona-fide* examples, when so many are faked. But which of our grandchildren will buy and frame the photographic group of a city syndicate, perched upon sticks, loader behind each gun, awaiting the four-figure flight of artificially reared birds ? What dealer will think it worth while to fake them ?

At one time the word " sporting " was prized by Englishmen as being untranslatable into inferior alien tongues ; now it has a slightly derogatory slant. It suggests a type of tweed and headgear, bounce and luxury. By luxury one does not imply expense alone, since there are many rigorous sports which cannot be enjoyed without cash or special opportunity. The lush element probably means going soft and letting others do the work and the thinking. Even the members of the expensive syndicate manage to aim and pull their own triggers, but the chronic crowds at professional matches pay a shilling to gape.

Salmon fishermen have by no means escaped the taint of luxury, but, taking all forms of fishing together, we may claim that no other sport has produced more followers able to fend for themselves, both in exercising their skill and in preparing their gear. If a complete reach-me-down standard outfit were to supersede the hand-built rod and the reel that needs normal manipulation, most of us would mourn the presumed gain as an actual loss. To pursue the wild thing in its appropriate natural setting, we need to rely, as far as is reasonable, on hand and eye. On where we draw the distinction between the simple and the elaborate depends the survival or the extinction of our sport.

Besides the advertised " improvements " with which super-applied science threatens our personal outfit, we shall have to submit increasingly to science unscientifically misapplied on our waters. The outlook in England is not good and every influence exerted towards saving the countryside will have to co-operate. Many of the most effective pioneers and workers for rural preservation regard blood sports as barbarous and cruel, as something to be bred and trained out—not encouraged. Thus a source of alliance is lost. However much we may prefer to slur it over, cruelty remains the black side of all sport, and the glib argument that because of it certain animals are pre-served, which would otherwise be exterminated, always seems to me to be a poor one. The Middle Ages might have said the same of the Jews. There is no logical answer to the taunt of cruelty, but there is, we may reasonably contend, a strong illogical mitigation. Sportsmen have done more than any other class to prevent wanton cruelty to animals. That is a matter of fact, not of opinion. Had there been a single sportsman among the heedless sailors on Mauritius, the dodo would not now be the by-word for the extinct. The primitive hunting side of man is still potent ; sport teaches him to realize that desire in the spirit of compassion and fair play. Can humanity to-day afford to neglect any popular recreation that fosters those qualities ?

In certain intellectual and artistic circles, where sport would be shunned, there is an admiration, amounting to a cult, for the neo-primitive. Here the sadistic elements of distortion and cruelty are accepted without repugnance. This is not the place to assess such values, but sport is an unbroken practice, which man has exercised throughout his history, and which he has learned to use socially. In my personal experience the few people I have met who have willingly attended a bull-fight have been intellectuals, not sportsmen. The apprehension of the sensitive will have its use if it tends to make us more scrupulous not to inflict unnecessary pain. Barbarous rituals, such as blooding the child who has witnessed his first kill out fox-hunting should repel anybody, though probably it is accepted without reaction by the child !

Fishing appears to give less offence than the pursuit of warm-blooded creatures, and fishermen are regarded by the unsympathetic rather as dotty, comical, or boring than as sadistic. The boring side probably arises from the habit of nurturing the sport at home. Shooters and hunters will also talk, but they don't spend their evenings making things and surrounded by clutter. Near and far relatives may admire the marvellous skill that they imagine to lie behind a salmon fly, but show them that triumph of care and ingenuity, a smooth worm hook mounted on nylon, and they will cringe.

It is, however, this zest for perfection, aroused by the angler, that turns its users into votaries. Nothing short of the ideal will do. Clumsy gear may catch fish and many fine exponents have had to " make do," but even tough professionals will spend precious time to achieve the precise colour, tone, and line of their flies, whilst the balance of mounts, leads, and spacing receive meticulous care. Those who can afford cash, or its equivalent time, insist on elegance and style. They have special items, like landing-nets, designed for them. People who do not themselves fish, but who still cherish their demented ones, appreciate that any gift connected with the passion will win unequalled response. Among such feats of affection I think the best is a little glass-shuttered opening, expensively inserted by a loving spouse, into the rear window of their car. When this opening is slid to one side the point of the full length trout rod sticks out of it—tailwise—in transit. When that car reaches the second-hand market, there will be a queue of applicants.

Books, pictures, and *objets d'art* connected with the angle acquire a fictitious presentation value. I have trudged vain miles seeking for a brass fish door-knocker. How often do I not lament that biological limitations debar me from the Flyfishers' Club and the consequent privilege of using its car mascot !

Through static centuries that fatted connoisseur, the Chinese mandarin, appreciated the art form of fishes, but, although he ate them—exquisitely—bred them, contemplated their grace, enjoyed their artistic range in ceramics and decoration, unlike the Sage, he himself rarely used the angle. This he left to the very young and to the lower orders. If he possessed the hereditary urge he may of course have humoured it by looking on, but he avoided a personal rôle. And yet is it so puzzling ? Even the most superb mandarin might survive disappointment in the competitive breeding of crickets, since the odium of second (or third) place might convincingly be explained away as due to the judge's ignorance or perfidy. The same mandarin would be only too well aware (from observing the very young and the lower orders) what might, or might not happen while fishing. How could so august a person sit creditably under a conspicuous umbrella, in the public gaze, for three blank days without exciting Opprobrium ? Those of us who have suffered know that even a graceful inscribed bamboo, a drift of silk line (from which is suspended a deftly carved float, and a golden hook bearing a succulent sweet-meat, sunk by a propitious jade) would not atone (to one of affluence and discernment) if the bamboo were unbloody and unbowed.

Face, Loss of, is not particularized in my massive dictionary of 1913. Its learned Scottish compiler may have regarded oriental sensibility as unworthy of his students. If so, there were not fishermen among them. It is humbling to have to confess how much this loss besets us, all of us and often ; however indignantly and virtuously we may try to disclaim it. Nobody really minds a blank day, or a series of blank days, if they occur as part-time recreation to oneself alone, and not in comparison with the fruitful bags of others. To have a made-up rod hanging in readiness in the back passage and something wet to cast into at the end of the back garden, would epitomize what we would ask for our last years. Just to go out alone for as short a time as we fancied, to cross the footbridge and feel the wind behind, to stay till the fish stopped feeding and return to begin our own ! Our characters would blossom with the triumphs won—and displayed—while losses would fall into philosophical perspective. We should be seen by our fellows in the round—dear old things ! But, put another man on the opposite bank !

After many years of experience, my own and the observations of others, I do not think there are many conceited fishermen, but the banks are paved with vain ones, uncertain and self-critical. Anyone joining a strange party—and in the years ahead we shall have to work more with strangers —should mind his step, if he wishes to placate and not provoke his companions. Fly-fishers will have to expect much more association and hotel water than private reaches. Only those of retired status are likely to be able to afford time to book with a pal for a long period. The wide range, lonely ramble will be hard indeed to find. It may appear a loss, but it should mean a compensation to many others to whom even a small share of these delights were previously denied. Parties will soon sort themselves out. For long some of the choicest fishing has been in the holding of clubs, and the companionship and experience gained there has been an enrichment, not a limitation. Friendly syndicates will be formed to rent private water and to pay for the vital protection and attention.

With overcrowding as it is, we could sympathize with men if they wished to block women out. Suppose, like cigarette-smokers and consumers of cocktails, we women

were to double the ranks of aspirants to scant waters?
Terrifying—yet I do not think we shall. I have always
been astonished by the kindness and encouragement which
men anglers thrust upon us. In spite of the noteworthy
forerunners (viz. Venus, Cleopatra, The Chou Empress of

VENUS AND CUPID

China, and Juliana), I have it on the excellent authority
of Alderman H. A. Hind, Honorary Secretary of the National
Federation of Anglers (representing a membership of a
hundred and fifty thousand coarse fishers) that only a very
few among them are women. Out of 680 invited to compete in the National Championship in 1945, only one woman
was selected. Women, so I understand, are better

represented in the large game fishing of the U.S.A. In these islands game fishing attracts a higher proportion of women than does coarse fishing, but, during the past twenty-five years new recruits are few. The array of martyrs who have constantly ministered to their angling males makes sad but elevating reading. Perhaps Plato has given the reason why they do not themselves join in—the sport is not sufficiently masculine.

In our discussions of the future and of possible developments I am only too well aware of my personal limitations. But to fear to tread is to rank oneself with the angels—even more presumptuous. In order to make it clear at the outset, and to avoid tedious safeguarding repetition, I must explain that latterly my own experience has been tethered to one beat on one salmon river (the Slaney, in South-East Ireland) and that observations on matters outside this range are from books, journals, and from what my friends have told me ; assisted by some long-distance recollections of strayings much farther afield. In this neutral island we have more than food to offer a bruised world and, although I sympathize with my own nationals who dread the over-crowding here that they already see on the waters of Patrick's Other Island, we can still extend a considerable welcome without ruinous congestion. There could be no better healing for society in its difficult convalesence.

During the worst years I used sometimes to feel that it was incongruous for me to spend an hour over the spin of a devon, when the world itself was whirling towards a vortex. I remember a day in September, 1940 : threshing was in full swing, but I left the busy yard in cynical disgust, fearful lest the grain won might be destined for an invader. I wandered towards the fountain, dried up—as such are in Ireland by even a fortnight's drought. The evening before three goldfish had still been living in the small pool that remained. I had forgotten to rescue them and at dawn a heron had been seen helping himself to the lot. I was furious. Then I despised myself for the loss in perspective shewn by minding. Was not the Battle of the Skies still in suspense ? I went back to the yard, to the pitch-forks of the men, and the kettles of the women preparing the threshers' dinner. Suddenly I realized that the world would not be normal again until small things, like the death of three goldfish, mattered in the balance of our lives.

CHAPTER II

ALAS! POOR FISH!

*" And now, where the bank gives easy access, a host
of spoilers are searching all the waters. Alas!
poor fish, ill sheltered by thine inmost stream!"*

THIS is not an apt quotation from a current copy of
The Field; it is taken from the Tenth Idyll of
Ausonius, *"Ad Mosellam"* (*c.* 310–393 A.D.).

The old problem has not lessened to-day. Consider the
strategic position of our Present Progressive and Future
Plu-Perfect times. There are, it has been assessed, at
least one million would-be anglers in Britain, and the
eventual improvement of transport must tend to increase
competition between them. How far could well-applied
engineering and knowledge of biology atone for what
science, recklessly misapplied, has already taken away?
How much can the banditry of Pollution, Poaching and
Power, the Three P's, be held in check or regulated?

It is not easy to write convincingly about the obvious,
and what could be more obvious than the horrible muddle
which has permitted the unnecessary waste by river pollution? Discussing it one trundles down the well-worn ruts
and finds that it has all been said, and done, before. Here
in Ireland the Liffey was once befouled by sewage. Very
few salmon would face up its mouth to run past Leixlip,
the town named by the Danes after the salmon. It proved
that Dublin was not as dirty as she is dear when, in
1906, the Corporation effected a notable purification in
their reformation of sewage disposal. As a result the river
regained normality in a few years time, without restocking;
surprisingly few fish are needed to renew the life-stream.

What could be done forty years ago could surely be achieved in other rivers to-day ? The Liffey, seen from O'Connell Bridge, still looks far from savoury, but salmon can put up with a lot of surplus decomposition if an undue amount of chemical effluent is not overcharged into the river's flow. The famous factories of Guinness, " J.J." whiskey, and Jacob's biscuits all flank its banks, but any discharge is properly neutralized. If they need an old-time illustration, dwellers by the Tyne and the Trent can point to the Liffey; since they—no more than fishermen—can really like the presence of so disgusting an intrusion.

Apart from monstrous abuses there are many dangerous smaller discharges, such as excesss protein from creameries, from sugar factories, flax or rettage (with the new method of re-using the same water for retting; damage from this source has become inexcusable). Certain effluents asphyxiate or sicken fish, others affect water vegetation and the prosperity of ephemera. We are learning that anything unnatural may lead to unforeseen disturbances of the life balance. Not only fishermen but people living away from the river's brink would benefit if towns and factories were forced to consume their own excreta.

Although in the past pollution has been the chief agent in destroying the sporting rivers of Britain, and has created a situation unlikely to be fully rectified, yet its future menace can be checked—if the public so desire it. Nobody, not even the factory owners or a local authority, really *prefers* smell or a nuisance, and there are known solutions which can be applied at a certain (but not at a prohibitive) cost. Æsop's fable of the lamb, drinking below the muddy disturbance made by the fox, is even truer to-day than when it was written, two thousand five hundred years ago. People are uninterested in those living downstream to them, and believe that their troubles are their own fault. Actually a person suffering from the effects of pollution created above him, and the consequent injury to his property, should take legal advice. Even if the trouble has been

created by a public authority, his defensive position is
stronger than many people realize. The recent activities
of the National Federation of Fisheries, of the British Field
Sports and the Pure Water Societies, in bestirring parlia-
mentary support, is being well backed by the most influential
of the press dealing with rural betterment, and should
show practical results. The best and simplest way for any
individual to join in the good work is to subscribe to those
bodies, or to some other that acts in co-operation. Game
fishers in Britain have the Salmon and Trout Association
(with headquarters at Fishmongers' Hall), and in Scotland
there is that effective body, the Scottish Salmon Angling
Federation. There is no excuse for anyone who proposes
to use his rod for not joining in. A few shillings subscribed
to the open hand are worth all the Jeremiads in the bush.

More insidious than the obvious ogre of pollution are the
supposed good fairy schemes, often only masquerading as
betterments. They sound so benevolent : water storage
for the new urban development (which will squeeze out the
moisture from the surrounding rural neighbourhood) ;
injudicious dredging and draining for the farmer, at the
expense of dried-up brooks and parched meadows. Above
all there is hydro-electric development, so drastic as to
merit a chapter to itself. Many of these projects are
launched with a high civic purpose ; to protest against
them would appear social treachery ; yet gradually the
streams and wells, which should nourish our rivers, are
sucked up and agricultural balance is dislocated. The loss
of volume of many streams represents a concealed revolution and has often created pollution, where the older ample
and more rapid flow was able to neutralize the offence.
Through weirs, or deepening and slowing the flow, more
silt accumulates above and the long extent of stagnant
water invites invasion by weeds.

This is not to say that no towns should be given water,
or land drained, but rural dwellers have the right to claim
that their district should not be mutilated without fore-

thought by single interests, public or private. Where water has had to be pumped or taken from a river, the only partial restitution is to put it back lower down. The naïve belief that a chalk stream was self-supporting through percolation from its banks has been the death of many of them, ruthlessly cut off from their wells and normal sources of supply. Why should the urban population be grossly favoured to the disadvantage of their rural neighbours? A country cottage with a hand-pump and earth closets consumes (i.e. wastes) enormously less per head than does a town house with uncontrolled taps and w.c.'s. Proper disposal and purification can, however, return the water borrowed at the upper reaches to the land on which the life of country dwellers depends. By using winter surplus and sparing, as far as possible, the normal sources, much unfairness could be mitigated.

No one expects that a project for general development is going to be held up because a few, even a great many, fishermen don't like it, but it is useful to remember that what fishermen may find out first may be thrust upon other country lovers and workers later. Sometimes the consequences may even react upon the towns which created them, who have robbed Peter in order not to pay Paulina. The hideous unnatural growth of industrialism to-day cries out to heaven, yet had anyone protested during most of the nineteenth century, he would have been put away in the name of the gold standard.

At present boards of various catchment areas, agricultural committees, and of rival Government departments, work independently. One can only hope that the Government Water Bill or the Regional Planning Authorities may achieve some co-ordination. It is understandable that some people, disgusted with " super-organization," now react even from Regional Planning ; yet the possibilities for consultation which are offered there should allay suspicion, since every interest is represented, and a full survey must be presented for inspection. If local anglers were to organize and anticipate possibilities, they could have an accurate brief ready. Nothing does more damage to a good cause than ignorant objections to imagined troubles. The Thames Conservancy Board has been subjected to much criticism for its dredging policy on the Kennet and elsewhere and it may have made mistakes, but it has spared no pains or research, and has often put up a good defence against misinformed abuse. The example of intelligent preparation made by the West Riding (Yorkshire) Fishery Board should give a lead to others. This Board maintains a system of files enabling it to note the pollution which has been detected in its area, while its automatic gauges record the flow of rivers under observation, and it can therefore supply precise information instead of vague speculation concerning the various catchment areas.

It is astonishing how little people appear to realize the limitations of waters they admire. Take the Shannon : it is seldom recognized that at its rosiest best, there were never more than fourteen miles (out of over two hundred) of regular spring fishing. Above Killaloe the water was always too deep for more than a casual take. Yet one still reads agitated appeals for " something to be done " to make the two banks of the two hundred miles " a salmon angler's paradise." The same type of claim is made for the Thames, if purified. The quality of Loch Leven depends upon the favourable geological nature of its bed, of the character of the rivers supplying it, and upon the balance of its depth. Yet a recent enthusiast has been writing in the press regretting that the Irish Government does not stock Loch Derg, which, he claims, should be ten times better than Loch Leven for trout because it is ten times bigger. It is the sort of remark that the caterpillar would attribute to Alice.

The existence of the Fresh Water Biological Society, at Wray Castle, Derwentwater, has now given a laboratory to the fisherman, and we can only hope that it may be enabled to extend its work. Even if it cannot solve all our problems, it can extinguish many foolish suggestions that might waste time and money. Ordinary fishermen cannot hope to understand the many complications involved in stock and river improvement. What we working rodsmen can do, is to use our eyes for observation, to value exact figures, and to keep our purses open to reasonable demands from those who are qualified to do the work for us. Blagdon is an example that new artificial works can provide new facilities, and the New Choke reservoir may do the same for Bristol. Some of these rays of hope will be discussed later, under " The Plus Sign."

In the coming battle for existence game fishers are more vulnerable, fewer in numbers, and less well organized than are the coarse-fish men, whose co-operation they sorely need. (I apologize for the use of the word " game " as a rough distinction from " coarse.") It may not be easy to persuade those latter well-equipped bodies that they have anything to gain by joining with the game fishers ; yet, without the full pressure of an effective membership of voters, the best results will not be won. The snob distinction between the two forms of the angle works largely to the disadvantage of the game-fish man, and that it should exist is partly his own fault. Salmon and trout have in England become the prerogative of the so-called upper classes. I understand that this is not so in Scotland. Salmon and trout waters are not only " strictly preserved," which, within limits, may be essential for preservation, but they represent an interest vested in far too few people, fishermen, and bank owners. The class consciousness is not wholly due to economics. I believe that very many of the coarse fishers could better afford to fish for trout than can the younger sons of younger sons, who still struggle to do so, and who would, if they failed, not bother to try a float. Again the Caterpillar might well say to Alice, " why should the spotted trout be pursued in a striped school tie, while the striped perch are spotted by the retailer and the artisan ? " To which Alice could only say she didn't know.

C

It may surprise some people to learn that on the Severn the coarse fisheries are worth more than the salmon interests.

If we agree that future pollution can in a large part be solved, and that drainage, water extraction, and storage reforms should at least be restricted to a fair measure of disturbance under expert guidance, we have still to face further illegal attacks upon our hardly-won prerogative. This trouble is one which the game fishers will have to fight alone, since for them market values dominate the position. If the salmon were only of the same commercial value as the mahseer, the situation would be easy indeed. Taking poaching in its progressive order of unpleasantness : (1) trespass with legitimate equipment ; (2) by gaffer or snatcher ; (3) by gangsters—the last is much the most damaging. The modern river thug works with explosive or poison, only using nets and gaffs to get his booty ashore. These methods not only deprive a river of its stock, but they cause widespread alarm and injury to the fish that may survive. Why conservators seem unable to enlist better police protection against these illegal acts is astonishing. Fishing by rod on another man's water is an affair of trespass, against which the owner can only take civil action to prove loss. To deplete a river or lake by illegal means is a recognized criminal offence. One has as much right to expect a reasonable anticipation of such acts, as one has to expect routine police patrols in a town and, to a lesser extent, in the country. Yet protection falls almost solely upon the private agents, employed by the conservators. The offenders, moreover, are among the very few criminals who are likely to retaliate by violence. The well wrought chain connecting them with their market starts with the provider of the explosive, the workers themselves find the nets and gaffs that may be needed on the spot, watchers look out for or placate local interests, special transport removes the booty to the chosen receiver. Salmon and sea-trout are such worth-while hauls that, until the value drops, the practice will repay the slight risk run by the perpetrators.

Undoubtedly inflated prices cause most of the trouble. Therefore, when I read of the immense encouragement given by the governments of Canada and the U.S.A. to increase the essential raw material of their salmon canning industries, my heart rejoices. I revel in the photographs of the teeming Sockeye salmon mounting the resuscitated Frazer River on their journey to the Middle-Cut. Not only canning, but improved chilling methods, will increase the quality and quantity of imported fish. If, in the off-points future, the housewife could obtain imported salmon much more cheaply, the price of the home article would drop. Normally, preserved food is not a subject to arouse enthusiasm from those who favour fresh products. In this instance, however, a plentiful and cheap supply might provide the best hope of our own salmon preservation. A serious drop in profits would not only slow down the organized thug, but it would curb the bloated and uneconomic prices gained recently by legitimate net fishing, which hinders an impartial river policy. Even a drastic drop in value would have no reaction on the normal rod fisher or upon rentals. To the rod-man the catch is a trophy, not a cash asset. The assessment of rod value, as compared to net value, is being worked out in detail in Canada, and would repay an objective survey in Britain.

When one deplores the apparent lack of police co-operation in countering large-scale depredation, one does not imply personal criticism of the unfortunate individual policeman. I do not know if those across the Channel are as much beset by social cares and responsibilities as are those pleasant young men comprising the Civic Guard in Eire. Here the local Sergeant in a country town is not only responsible for the prevention of crime and disorder in his district, he is also the Authority from whom one obtains ration cards (original or lost), to whom one has to " furnish " those intimate personal revelations without which one could not (during the most critical period of poaching) obtain a compassionate permit to visit one's sick parent in England; he is the appropriate official who must oversee the destruction of obnoxious weeds, take precautions against animal diseases, breaches of dog or wireless licences, absence of lights on bicycles, and the presence of illicit passengers in bread vans; he must attend for extra duties at athletics, he must, etc. etc. At the close of day, after licking his last envelope, can he be blamed if he resists the urge to take a precautionary prowl along the cold river bank? Were I he, it would be sausages and a chair every time.

This extra duty is, like many other tasks of rural conservation, becoming too complex for the range of the regular over-taxed police. If in Ireland we had a special rural police corps to cover the protection of wild life (including trees and flowers), of orchards and other subjects for youthful sabotage, of birds and game, even of the encroachment of ivy throttling our trees, it would repay a grant from the substantial funds allotted to the Irish Tourist Board. Sport is a recognized asset for visitors: all hotel-keepers will agree that long-term residents are not held by a recreational menu of scenery alone. Some such protective policy was recommended by those responsible for the report on which many of the excellent provisions of the 1939 Irish Fisheries Act was based. At that time the suggestion did not appeal to the government, but since then the prospects of the tourist future have brightened, while at the same time the menace to our main attractions has increased. No other panacea is worth anything if protection is neglected.

Because large-scale illegal raidings are so much more important, one cannot ignore the trespass nuisance, against which owners and lessees must protect themselves. Even the bailiff employed by the Board of Conservators is not permitted to interfere with any person fishing legally anywhere. He may give the hint to the injured party and the fact that the offender has been seen may cramp his style. This form of offence varies in intensity with the district, and is more likely to occur on waters loosely preserved for trout and coarse fish than on exclusive salmon banks. The bane of the salmon fisher is more often the supposed " liberty " for trout or coarse fishers to roam over his beat. There are few owners who are such curmudgeons as to interfere where salmon do not lie. This is different to a general catch-as-catch-can permission to all. The range of the motor-bicycle increases the scope of strangers and, were a general privilege exercised, those fishing for salmon would be intolerably handicapped. On a Bank holiday I have seen certain upper reaches of the Slaney crowded with trout fishermen, insisting on unconfirmed " permission." They ignore the non-wading convention, which those who control only one salmon bank must observe ; they kill smolts or chuck them back carelessly ; as often as not they use long two-handed rods, with which they rake the river from bank to bank.

To counter this nuisance creditably there is no better protection than allowing local neighbours to trout fish, if the owner's party are not themselves occupying the water. It is far better to be served by unpaid keepers than to play dog-in-the-manger.

Deliberate gate-crashers on trout and other waters, held by associations and clubs are extremely difficult to forestall, and their existence adds to the expense of those who pay to fish there. It is impossible for each member to recognize an undesirable alien on sight ; nothing but the employment of a permanent keeper during the season will protect legitimate interests.

From time immemorial a latent sympathy has been with the gaffer or snatcher. The cruelly harsh sentences that were said to be imposed in the days of old-fashioned " J.P.'s " for trivial offenders are now often replaced by a trifling fine. Apart from romantic sympathizers for the poacher, there are many more people of the something-for-nothing type, who help to make the practice of the privateer profitable. Such persons consider themselves wholly respectable ; they include " honest " business men and even clergy, who would bitterly resent larceny from their own cash or alms-boxes ; yet they will gladly trade in anything just out of season if they can get it cheap. People who would not break the law (except the customs) have no compunction at paying others to do it for them. This public failing lies at the root of most of the endemic poaching in Ireland.

Fishermen too, before they condemn the odd man with a quick gaff, would do well to remember how deteriorating it must be to owe your living to odd day's earnings, tips, and pickings. The old solution of employing doubtful characters to keep off others—on the principle of the Indian *Chowkedah*—may answer in the right place, if it gives regular employment. Off-season maintenance of boats, piers and stands should encourage the creation of a better class of gillie ; it is unlikely to alter the old hand, or to deter a deliberate type of enterprise ; yet the existence of chronic parasitic service can only react upon the sportsmen who trade upon it, and upon the quality of the sport by maintaining a larger reservoir of shady characters.

CHAPTER III

WHITE POWER POLITICS

EVERYTHING that reduces available water makes fishing more difficult and expensive. Recently the distinguished bodies responsible for the establishment of hydro-electric schemes have expressed more concern for the unfortunates to be dispossessed by their activities than was at one time thought worth while. How far this solicitude is actual or nominal must be left for the victims to assess, but there is little doubt, apart from the question of personal compensation, that great thought is now being given to the future—if any—of the local fishery interests.

The River Erne in Ireland, and what is called the Pitlochry Scheme (a far more vast affair), in Scotland, are the two outstanding works ahead and in progress. Had not the coal situation intensified the need for more power, it is possible that all this hydro-electric enterprise might not have appeared as desirable as it seems to-day. Water power, even when there is a good fall and an assured flow, has repeatedly proved not only to be disruptive, but also an economic disappointment. So great an authority as the late Sir Charles Parsons himself told me (speaking before the 1939 war) that he hardly knew of one that had fully justified the vast capital upheaval, and the unforeseen incidental complications. But that is neither here nor there. Our interest lies in the fishing reactions, of which some general ideas may be gained from the experience of the Shannon Scheme and the Liffey works, both in operation under the management of the Electricity Supply Board (E.S.B.) of Eire. The outstanding lesson revealed by these examples is that, no matter how sensible and solicitous may be the " alleviations prescribed," a good river is not

going to recover a shock that undermines its system.
The patient may regain a little strength, even learn to
foster an alternative interest, but its glory has departed,
blasted by an outrage to its balance, constitution, and
rhythm. The Shannon has probably suffered less fatally
in its gross salmon run than would many others because of
the generous tributaries, such as the Mulcair, the Maigue
—passing through Adare—and the Fergus, that feed its
estuary below the dam ; also because the main spawning
beds were always situated low down ; Castleconnell is only
just above the estuary, and running fish can still reach the
main redds even in thin water. Comparison of the river's
catch is necessarily difficult to assess accurately, since it
has to be made between an uncertain past and a definite
present. Every fish that passes through is now counted.
The official export figure (pre-Siemens Schuckert) could not
have revealed more than a relative estimate of the annual
run. Nets, legal and illegal, raked its waters, and the rod
catches at Castleconnell had dropped dramatically even
before the German invasion. Mr. John Rennie, writing in
the " Lonsdale " Library (*Salmon Fishing, p.* 410), says,
" Looking up old records I find that away back (in 1865,
the beat known as Doonas, at Castleconnell, killed 425) . . .
in the year 1866, 671 salmon and grilse . . . from 1889
to 1892 the average catch on Doonas is about 35 salmon
up to the end of May, and in 1889 only 19 fish were
caught."

From 1920 to 1930 the position was somewhat better,
but nothing like the really good old days before the intense
commercial netting began. After the E.S.B. took on the
management of the fisheries in 1935, all netting and rod
fishing was suspended for five years, in order to give the
stock a breather for recovery, so 1941 marks the first year
of recorded figures. I have to thank Mr. Liam Forde,
Manager of the Fisheries, for the following particulars :

FISH ACTUALLY CAPTURED

Year.	Thomond Weir Weight	4-Stake Weirs Weight	Total Weight
1941 -	55,655 lbs.	Not working	— —
1942 -	47,570 ,,	61,145 lbs.	108,715 lbs.
1943 -	39,463 ,,	58,550 ,,	98,013 ,,
1944 -	25,756 ,,	28,570 ,,	54,326 ,,
1945 -	12,903 ,,	10,517 ,,	23,420 ,,
1946 -	18,780 ,,	7,892 ,,	26,670 ,,

" In 1941 and 1942, 33⅓ per cent. of the total run of salmon which passes through Thomond Weir were captured, and during the subsequent seasons 28 per cent. The proportion of grilse was as follows :

1944	- -	77 per cent.
1945	- -	74 per cent.
1946	- -	82 per cent.

" . . . Everyone must be only too well aware that the downward trend in the run of salmon, as set out in the foregoing, was experienced in practically every river in England, Ireland, Scotland, Norway, and to a certain extent in Canada."

We may agree with Mr. Forde that those bad years are a matter of general history, but we may anyhow congratulate the E.S.B. for a policy which allowed so high a proportion of fish to go through during the worst period. Whether the bad takes were due to ocean perversity or to the admittedly dry, cold springs has yet to be settled by our experts. It must, however, be noted that the Shannon was even more adversely affected by the reduced flow than were normal rivers because of the unusual demands made upon the turbines. Coal imports were so severely restricted that electricity had to be rationed to a twinkle ; it was not possible to increase the statutory flow of ten cubic metres per second that passes through the gate at O'Brien's Bridge, where the head race starts. Judging only by the appearance of the sadly-depleted river, it was generally doubted whether even this allowance was actually maintained. It is essential to take note of these extra adverse factors before deciding that the Shannon is finally lost as a salmon river for rods. Mutilated, yes, but the rising graph of the grilse take, which immediately responded to the wet summer of 1946, gives cause for hope, especially when taken in conjunction with the power bestowed by a policy of single control from redd to ocean. The increase in the proportion of the grilse run, apparently at the expense of large springers, is often laid at the door of the hydro-electrical development. Possibly the charge is badly framed and should run that while big fish are reluctant to move up into depleted waters, the grilse are fortunately less suspicious, and so something is left. I prefer, however, the explanation that grilse runs rise and fall in cycles, and that the marked rise in this run in the Shannon reflects a general tendency that had reached a climax in 1946. The rod total was extremely low during the war years, with very few fishers, but a considerable proportion of the take ran to between 26 and 34 lb. Mr. Forde tells me that a large number of fish sulked in the long, deep stretch of water below Castleconnell, that was previously disturbed by the Abbey Guild of netmen ; apparently the fish do not now run upstream to meet the rods. This new unnaturally natural peace, combined with the absence of flood impetus, may well have produced inertia and left them latent until the late autumn. If this be so, one imagines that so electric a body as the E.S.B. may have some galvanic shock up its sleeve for use on a future occasion.

Our two Irish examples have made it clear—were proof needed—that fish will not run from the ocean unless there is the impetus of sufficient bouts of fresh water at the right time and of the needed temperature, at the estuary and at the river's mouth. Without this summons, reaching far out to sea, salmon will not receive the call of the river (known scientifically as the gradient of salinity) that they left as smolts. It had been generally surmised, and was proved dramatically by the tagged fish of Dr. A. Huntsman of Canada, that they prefer their original home, even after wandering 1,000 miles away from it in the ocean. But not so nostalgically that they will not go next door if their own bell is not ringing. In 1944 and 1945, when the raped Anna Liffey failed to attract her offspring back to her depleted bosom, they ran up quite small neighbouring rivers, though few survived to gladden their foster-mothers.

There remains the hope that what a river has lost on the salmon swings the trout may gain later on the roundabouts of the upper waters. The Liffey, which is also a water-storage scheme, converted acres of land into lake, whereas the Shannon dam only deepened the vast existing waters of Loch Derg. Before the establishment of the dam, the upper Shannon and certain tributaries, such as the Brosna, above Banagher, and the Suck, by Ballinasloe, gave occa-sional rich openings to those living locally, who understood the special conditions likely to bring up salmon. These conditions did not provide steady seasonable runs, but (in common with most tributaries to big rivers) were largely dependent upon early autumn freshes and coloured water to attract fish, but at favoured times residents enjoyed much delightful sport. Above Loch Derg fish were often taken at Banagher, and the run would proceed through the beautiful expanse of Ree, above Athlone, as far as Loch Allen in County Leitrim. Salmon rarely fell to a rod on the lakes, but were taken in nets working for coarse fish. Since the dam was formed the loss to salmon-fishers above it has been absolute, despite the existence of an effective ladder connecting the old river with the upper water and which the autumn fish use freely. Up to 1946 nothing was caught in the Brosna nor the Suck, nor in the main river at Banagher ; in despair many people have criticized the policy of the E.S.B. in concentrating upon the passage of the old river, instead of providing a " hoist " to by-pass it at the turbines. Fish, they maintain, must prefer to run into the fuller flow of the tail-race rather than to mount the reduced flow of the old river. At first sight this objection would appear reasonable ; if the solution of establishing a hoist would produce a happy issue out of their afflictions and still leave enough stock to furnish Castleconnell. Unfortunately, the radical changes which the dam has brought to the river make it most unlikely that even an earlier run up past the turbines, through the head race, would cure the troubles in the tributaries. I use the word earlier advisedly because there is no doubt at all that a very large number of fish do mount the ladder and eventually reach the upper redds. This is not a matter of opinion ; it is a fact. The proof is there in the watching. Anyone who visits the wide head-race in April can watch the multitude of eager smolts racing along the thirty-five yards of vibrating grid that repels their passage through the turbines. When the turbines are closed down to admit navigation, the smolts are directed into the navigation lock (large enough to hold a big barge) the water seethes with the silver streaks that are passed down to continue their next phase of perilous life. According to Mr. Forde, there was a record smolt run in 1946, and the next best the previous season.

Constant observation of the tail-race, supported by netting, has discredited the theory that spawning fish remain in it instead of mounting the old course. They may rest there awhile, but only an inconsiderable fraction remain and fail to mount the old course. Not more than from 60 to 300 fish in one year have been proved to stay and spawn in the race. In dry seasons the turbines are shut down at night, aud the sudden cessation of current induces the salmon to fall back and then mount the river with even less delay.

Accepting the biological necessity for parents, we shall have to admit that adult salmon must have ascended the ladder and have spawned in the upper waters. The plight of sportsmen above Loch Derg would appear to be derived from the culminating factors of physical changes in level and flow. I have seen a letter from a resident on the Brosna deploring the absence of the big brown trout which used to run up from the main river in the autumn (as I know well from personal experience). Such trout, like the salmon, are clearly reacting from profound local provocation.

It must also be remembered that the Shannon has only begun to recover from the blast to its stock. The appalling losses before 1935 especially affected the upper waters, from which for several years practically no smolts could reach the sea. The present easy transit has only been working since 1940. The rhythm of return has not had time to be fully established and a natural restoration may develop. Moreover, with more normal spring weather and possibly a flush or two of extra water now and then past the dam down the old river, fish might mount earlier. In Mr. Rennie's chapter he comments on how few spring fish ever passed Killaloe. For the rod, the grilse run is likely to offer the best hope in the summer, with the odd big ones to sweeten the spring. Concerning the trout, it seems difficult not to believe that when natural readjustments have been made to the increased depth, the change of verge, and the decreased velocity in flow, that the old habit of running up in the early autumn to spawn later will not return. The future enemy to the Shannon tributaries would appear to lie in misapplied dredger drainage.

The other martyr to Irish power policy is the Liffey. Again, it is too soon to assert positively that the loss is absolute, in view of the exceptional dry seasons early in 1945 and 1946. The very wet summer of 1946 should have given encouragement to the late run if present. This river is one of the few that attracts a run of some fresh fish all the year round, although admittedly the spring run used to predominate. Probably it was this obliging feature that saved her life in the polluted days preceding 1906.

The spawning beds have always lain below the dramatic waterfall of Poulaphouca now harnessed to Moloch, and so a mounting ladder was not needed. Unlike the Shannon, whose turbines need a considerable volume of water to atone for the absence of fall, the Liffey relies upon fall. The land that was inundated was flat, often boggy, but agricultural, and the great extent submerged (up to nine square miles) was largely determined by Dublin's need for water. Geologists tell us that originally the area formed part of an inland sea, bounded by lower hills on the north and west, and by the fine bluff of Dublin mountains on the east. The work of inundation involved one very small extra expense that would not have occurred outside Ireland. The local inhabitants working for the English engineering company who carried out the scheme refused to fell the venerated " lone thorns " growing on the projected bed of the new lake. During the war years it was not easy to import sacrilegious strangers with axe and saw, and one could see these isolated but doomed trees, standing, " lone," indeed, after all other species had fallen. Even so, a few must have been overlooked, as, driving from Blessington several years after the inundation, one can still see on the left-hand side some uneasy top branchlets peering out of the water. (I have not heard whether they have been the cause of a lost trout.)

The responsibility of this scheme was shared by the E.S.B. with the Dublin Corporation, which needed a vast increase in addition to the Roundwood reservoir, supplied by the soft waters of the Vartry. Despite the size of the new lake, the need to conserve every drop of water is urgent. Were the demands of the turbines alone to be met, the height of the fall would have sufficed with comparatively little flow, and a good surplus would have reached the river to operate the two additional stations below Poulaphouca. The summer demand for water, however, is so great that in the winter the re-charge seldom exceeds its limited allowance to flush the estuary. In this scheme, however, what was lost to the salmon-fishers might, it was hoped, be more than compensated by gain above to many trout-fishers. The area has a good alkaline content and the Liffey and

PONLAPHONCA NEW LAKE

LOCH DERG OF THE MAY-FLY

other brooks entered it to supply its needs from the Dublin mountains, and maintain spawning grounds. These streams had an abundant supply of the small trout common to acid waters. It is well known that the first few years following an inundation are abnormally good, but there was every reason to hope that if care were taken to control the number of trout and to help the stock of natural feeding that a more sustained result might be achieved. The Department of Fisheries gave every help and the E.S.B. were advised by experienced experts. In 1940 the filling began and by 1942 the real fun started.

It is no fishing exaggeration to say that tons of trout were taken by rod (and possibly by other engines) during 1942 and 1943 ; and not numbers alone, but fat lumps of superb trout, up to 5 lb. in weight. The little fellows from the upper brooks rushed into the rich feeding-ground of the lake. Only lack of transport—twenty-five miles from Dublin—limited the ecstasy. Most of the sport was restricted to the bank. Some of the fly-men expressed disapproval over the activities of " tooth-pickers—" many of them commercially casting over a wide range of water and pricking more fish than they landed. I know, however, that those advising the Board were anxious to see the surplus stock of trout reduced before the inevitable drop in food supply set in, and that there was no serious objection to the thread-liners. To some of us, however, it was good to know that far the highest score fell to the fly, or perhaps it would be fairer to say to the outstanding accomplishment of one man who tied his own and cast them so beautifully. In the legend of these glorious days the name of Mr. Richard Harris will always stand out. He is not only an expert man behind a rod, but his knowledge of fauna and ephemera has aptly won him a place on the demonstration staff of Trinity College, where he lectures on limnology. Dick has every trick in the bag, and he will pull out any one of them —along with the trout. His method of standing well back from the verge of the lake and then of dropping his cast just beyond dry land, near to where the fly was hatching out, was an affair of artistry.   In the two seasons of '42–'43 Dick Harris, fishing in the evenings only and not every day, landed 18 cwts. of trout on his nine-foot rod.   A friend who accompanied him on two evenings on the Liffey, above the lake, told me that he himself was getting a few, but he had to stop to watch Dick.   He had never more than two flies up, often only one, and he cast a long line dead across to the opposite bank.   He would bring it in fairly fast.   On those two evenings my friend helped him to carry home 60 lb. weight of trout, averaging 2 lb.   No man could be more generous in giving flies or advice, but unluckily he cannot hand over his artistry, which extends to the capture of salmon, or to anything else that swims. In justice to tooth-pickers, I must admit that a worthy second place was filled by a Belgian expert in that genus. Since Harris is no lover of the thread-line, it caused keen amusement when, as a reward in a fly-casting competition, he was presented with the latest type of multiple-geared reel.

The climax had, however, no sooner been reached when a horrible day arrived.   A trout was found with a long and unpleasing tapeworm in its gut.   The lake, as we have mentioned, is now the main supply of Dublin's drinking water, and the department in charge at the corporation had more than a *mauvais quart d'heure*.   Some types of these odious objects may be conveyed to humans.   Mercifully, this variety (*Diphyllobothrium*) prefers the trout, but in case its cousins might be about, all fishing was closed down and a period of intense research was begun under Dr. M. D. Hickey, assisted by Dick Harris.   Until their report is published it would be fatuous to speculate on cause or cure.   It is known that the macabre life cycle requires an adult host, say a gull or cormorant ; from the excreta of the bird passes the first element of its life which is consumed by the water shrimp or flea on which the trout in turn feeds. The worm then develops inside the trout, which is once more eaten by the adult host. Thus the cycle is renewed. Presumably it would help if the birds were killed off—but think of the number around that huge lake and the immense sources for renewal! This type of worm was, I understand, once present in South Wales. There were two varieties in Poulaphouca, only one of which was fatal to trout. Most unpaying guests prefer not to kill their unwilling hosts. Pondering this event, so rare in its incidence, one wonders how far these stupendous alterations of natural features may not contain the source of abnormality from which strange visitations might arise. . . . On the other hand, we must not overlook the offence given to the Lone Thorn.

The fishing was re-opened in 1945 and the stock has been much reduced in number and in size. Rentals are not high and are by day or by the season. It is hoped that an average of ¾ lb. may make fishing worth while to visitors both on the lake and in the Liffey above it. Owing to fears of casual pollution, boats are not encouraged, but slight concessions are made to residents. One of my friends, with a house near the shore, wished for leave to bathe and asked for an application form. It came, written in both Irish and English. Before permission to bathe in the lake could be granted to his household my friend had to make a solemn declaration that neither he nor they would take advantage of the " facility " by attempting suicide by drowning.

Gulls still flock in their thousands. The comparatively recent change of habit in the so-called sea-gull is disturbing. Attracted by the easy booty of the land, these new mar-auders invade first the estuaries, charging down on herring shoals, or, so it is feared, smolts, proceeding upstream to upset once again the precarious balance of power. The scavenger of garbage rarely remains satisfied with his lowly portion ; he discovers richer flesh-pots in the little rivers and by the shores of lakes. That he should also combine the attributes of an " adult host " is a ghastly corollary, one for which human interference can for once not be

D

blamed. The trout admittedly are there and so are the less harmful of the worms, which appear to make little difference to the trout's condition. Curiously enough, women remain unconvinced by the assurance of the scientists that the affected trout make delicious eating.

About the other threats to our Irish rivers : Lock Erne is in the course of being harnessed, with what prospect of salmon survival or of trout improvement I do not know, but the feeling is pessimistic. After that, what else ? The historic Boyne has been severely threatened and measured, but so far it has, I understand, shown itself to be wholly unco-operative. The Slaney, too, has had its alarming visits by surveyors, the establishment of water gauges, and so forth, but we pray that its once-deplored quality of fizzling out after a fortnight's dry spell in summer (and the fact that the appropriate place for a dam is at least six miles from the nearest town) may save our salmon and the inundation of much valuable land. The Lee at Cork, alas ! is believed to be the next victim.

The future of our rivers, here as elsewhere, rests upon precarious foundations. No one really knows what will happen to anything, or what revolutionary possibilities lie ahead. If the coal export from England to Ireland does not recover, alternatives will have to be sought locally. Turf utilization on the site for electrical generation is freely discussed. Every country must dread dependence upon power purchased from overseas. Equally, the risk of expending capital and of destroying existing assets—on projects that may soon be out-dated—are not lightly to be undertaken.

It is good to know that in Scotland responsibility for the non-profit-making Pitlochry Scheme have taken the counsel of Mr. W. L. Calderwood, a key-name among fishery experts. He has made every possible effort to improve the arrangements to favour the salmon, and even when all could not be won, the worst undoubtedly was mitigated, especially in averting the submersion of spawning beds. At

Tongland in Galloway he followed the smolts' unexpected reactions from the surge tower to and through the turbines. Strange as it may seem, instead of being minced, they don't mind at all. When run at full load the turbines allow ample room for the fish to pass through without injury by the vanes. At Pitlochry, however, the smolts would also have to face pressure of over 50 lb. owing to the height of the 165' 0" fall. Would they survive this ordeal? A testing apparatus was set up by the engineers under Mr. Calderwood's guidance and the small fish stood up to an artificial pressure of 70 lb.; after this they lay down, but revived quickly. They did not turn a hair at the estimated Pitlochry pressure, nor show any subsequent internal reactions. With all the wise precautions taken, we may hope that some of those rivers comprised in the system, which are to be spared the worst of the upheaval, may still show sport, and that enough salmon will be there to mount the interesting roomy orifices forming the pools of the model substitute for a ladder. Will enough flow be spared from the equalizing reservoir to urge them up? I know nothing of the other possibilities that these new expanses of water may bring to trout-fishers, but we may be quite certain that the local Scotsmen are wide awake. We can only wish them very well through the varied twists and tursn that are inevitable in what Vitruvius has called "the meanderings of water."

CHAPTER IV

TWO SEASONS

AFTER discussing such important matters one begins
to feel an urge for the open-air and the bending rod
To do so is to risk losing constructional form, since there
still remain many strategic aspects which would more fitly
round off the chapters that have preceded this one. A well-
planned book on fishing may be a thesis on some particular
technique ; it may be a work of reference, or it may recall
the memories of one who has loved and practised it. Here
we shall only attempt an appraisal of the recent past, into
which the present so quickly merges. From it we may
better be able to hazard some forecast of what is likely to
happen to-morrow. In such a mixed fishing-bag there need
be no set order ; we will put a hand inside and pull out
the tins, selecting those that our fingers touch. We know
their shape so well that we do not need to recognize their
colours ; a hotch-potch, may be, but if so then only the
more like our fishing talks, where argument—darting to
and fro—will change sides and subject every minute.

For the moment we may ignore the tins inside our bag
and instead look into the outside pocket, where—if we
are lucky—we may find a fish itself. A fish with me will
almost surely be a salmon, caught on one river. I shall
not again apologize for this limitation because had I more
actual data I should probably get confused. After all,
long ago I wandered fairly far ; now I can always read or
listen about other rivers, even visit them without a rod.
But to relish comparisons and chew the cud, I have come
to prefer a familiar haunt. Obviously as one gets older it
is natural to feel at home in one's own chair rather than
in the more handsome upholstery offered by a hotel.

Our bit of water—about three-quarters of a mile of one bank—is augmented by some stands rented immediately above us, and we frequently fish the opposite bank too. Thus in 1945 we covered one and half miles, two sides, and in 1946 we had a further three-quarters of a mile above us (one bank). We lie about twenty miles above tidal water and the river is rapid with a rocky or cobbled bed, with a width of some thirty yards, averaging 3' 6" to 4' deep. Our season is best during March to the end of May, and fizzles out in mid-June. Actually I have had some lovely days later in the summer before the close on August 31st, all the more delightful because there was no commercial tension attaching to them.

In the spring of 1945 the Emergency was pressing hard upon transport. There was no alternative to a bicycle or trap, and it was increasingly hard to secure visitors. We are fortunate in that our house is only a mile from the fishing cabin, and I was therefore determined to accept the last minute offer of my *vis-à-vis* to rent me the bank opposite, although I could only muster a couple of regular rods.

Apart from our familiar house-party, which traditionally assembles for the opening three days (the last three days of February), the rods were myself, Denis (butler in his few leisure moments) and, when available, FitzPatrick (herd and agricultural worker, in his leisure moments). A few itinerant friends joined in from time to time. Shortly after the opening quite unforeseen and saddening circumstances took me away from the river, and for the rest of the season what fishing I did was only in snatches. However, a young invalid from the forces was able to spend his convalescnece with us, and the beneficial river life soon enabled him to do gallant service for the bag. Although a comparative novice to the salmon, he quickly borrowed skill from Denis, and, moreover, he joined competently in the home-made gear-works on which we all so greatly rely.

So much for our personnel. Generally speaking, 1945 was not a good season, but with us February had been mild with good water, and when we opened we found that fish were up. We started off with seven on the opening day, all caught on our own wooden devons. We kept up a fair average until the middle of a rather cold March. Undoubtedly 1945 and 1946 were unduly favourable for our beats. During both years in early February good water had encouraged fish to mount, but the temperature was not so warm as to hurry them through. We seemed to maintain a steady stock throughout both seasons. So far from being too warm or too high in 1946, the weather in early March was excruciatingly cold (after March 1st we caught nothing for a fortnight), then a flood came and obligingly lifted fish from the beats lower down. Few ran through, even to our upper end, even new-comers lingered with us until someone managed to pull them out. Although less fish entered the river's mouth in 1945 than in 1946, the rods everywhere had better sport that year and our numerically weak team took 179. In 1946, with more rods and more water, we had 144, but that year our neighbours both above and below were worse off still, so by comparison we were even luckier than we were in 1945.

I labour these details because they may give an understandable background for the lessons and observations we gained. To start with, in 1945 Denis had better scope than he usually has, and one was able to form a real opinion on many details that might otherwise have been put down to coincidence or to differing personal skill. Reference to the table, p. 188, will better illustrate the effect of Denis's example. Well-stocked rivers, like the Moy, where some fish are always present, differ from ours, dependent upon less stock and new supplies. Usually one can never say definitely whether on a given day there are fish present, certainly not fresh ones. Therefore one is apt to exaggerate or depreciate the results of one's methods. In 1945 our data was comparatively opulent ; we could judge whether a sequence was accidental or reasonable. For instance, we landed 15 consecutive cocks—clearly identifiable.

Another year (before the ladies had righted the balance) I might have written to *The Field* solemnly suggesting a reason. It did not take us long in 1945 to realize that a " run on the red " can happen with anything, without any reason. People who lose, say, nine fish running (" they just came unstuck ") can become unbelievably boring when they bleat about it, suggesting explanations. But not so boring as the smug person who has landed nine running, and who tells you exactly how he is presenting his fly and times the hand to follow the eye—which sounds like poetry. Possibly fish may sometimes see better than they appear to do at other times, but far more likely " the red "—or " the black "—is running again.

We may accept the dictum that any fool can catch a salmon and that on some days no one can, yet I also remember my first day with a trout fly—a dry one, too— on the Wiltshire Avon, where trout are much more wary and choosey than are the accompanying grayling. I had been given two flies, and I admit it was to my credit that it took me a morning to flick off one of them. Too eager to wait for the evening rise, I slipped out again in the grilling August sun—clad in white tennis gear. Standing bolt upright, I saw a rise, miraculously plopped the "alder" within range and had him on. I remember fortifying myself by repeating " he's only like a perch " as I steered him round the banks of weeds. I had no net, but scooped him out with my hand and executed him with a blow from my tennis shoe. I ran spread-eagle to the house, rod in one hand and—still attached to the cast—a 17-ouncer in the other.

Yes, a fool may catch a trout or a salmon, but, as one of medium class, I find it mortifying to realize how many more a better man can land than oneself. Previously it had been masked for me, since—as our butler—Denis had other irrelevant demands upon his time ; consequently I always had the best bits first. Still arriving later than the rest of us that year, he had a free range, and he stayed out till nightfall. His bag was 76 (out of the 179), and we

averaged four rods during the best of the season. To gain
consistently better results than your fellows is not the
reward of dexterity alone ; the good killer has the skill
to carry out what he wants to do, but he does not give
way to the temptation of letting his skill run away with
him. He uses it, but he will not minister to it. Denis is
more interested in the fish than in his own technique. It
is not, as people have suggested, only a matter of knowing
his water well and so wasting no time. I must know it
quite as well, but I am more fearful of wasting time. When
I watch him I am amazed not at his selection of a good
spot, but at the care with which he will comb out every
inch of water where he has ever known a fish at that height
to be. If I am over-enthusiastic or tired I am inclined to
hop and go one. My rosier hunches may sometimes be
good, but my sombre patches will hurry me past the spots
where Denis will follow me later more slowly—to wipe
my eye. This quality of persistently working for one's
fish is what has most impressed me during these past two
seasons. It is, of course, based on confidence, itself rooted
in reason. Guileless optimism can be annoying, and once
it has been exploded it will destroy future confidence.
Feeling cynical and experienced, how often our party has
twitted Denis for staying out late when we were going
home ? We prattle of how it is too cold, too hot, too high,
too low, too misty, too sunny—above all, how there are
no fish. Off goes Denis (with the subdued politeness I
have only seen elsewhere in a bishop's secretary) to the
right place at that hour. It is a fact that by the end of
1946 not one of our party would lay a bet against his getting
a fish even on what appeared to us the worst type of evening.
Of course, he did not always pull it off, and he is curiously
subject to horrible misadventures, but the force of his
example upon the rest of us, I am sure, helped more than
any other factor in keeping our tails up and our lines wet.
The factor of morale may be a well-known one, but it is
never trite.

Unlike the pseudo-scientists with printed tables, thermometers, barometers, polarized glasses and river gauges, Denis relies on his native arts and hands. He has made us a river gauge and we usefully record its readings in our register, but I know that he prefers his familiar marks on rocks and so forth awaiting him at useful tactical points. After all, you can't carry the main gauge away with you, and if you allow yourself to become hidebound to the mechanical aid you may easily neglect those clues which nature offers to those who have eyes to notice them. Like all men of imagination, Denis has his superstitions, often, I consider, unfounded. Sometimes he will abandon them, but quite often I have to confess that Denis may have been admiring what I have come to believe the right thing for the wrong reason ! At one time he would only use natural baits, and he shivered if an artificial lacked eyes or other biological addenda. Gradually in 1945 he began to believe in the wooden devon (painted surrealistically by me), and by 1946 he preferred then to any other. He had evolved his own method, abandoning slow and deep even for quite cold water (really low temperatures are rare with us) ; he uses two flat leads weighing between one-third to half an ounce, usually lighter. These he fishes fairly fast, beginning to reel in as soon as they have touched the water. It took me some time to realize that, except in very strong water, he never puts on more lead with these light baits, although he changes the size of the bait very often. If there is one slogan bait fishers have been taught to revere it is fish high or fish deep, but avoid the middle water. Even with light leads Denis's baits are suspiciously near middle water ; in our shallow stream we have very few deep holes. Should one decide to discard slow and deep as a constant spring slogan it would, I am sure, be equally foolish to substitute the opposite as a fixed policy. There are times and places where one must fish deep and slow—but the more we drop the misleading word *always* the better. Whatever may be the ultimate merits of the depth, there is no question that one loses far fewer baits with light leads, and as, since following Denis's policy, I find they catch me more fish, I have discarded heavy ones, except in really high, fast water.

To steady the bait in really rapid water is not an affair of lead alone. Something beefier is needed. Wooden baits can become hysterical ; I have given some of them skimpier vanes and then added a spiral ribbing of seal's fur to the bodies, using the plan shown on page 84, Fig. 1. They behave most creditably under false fire at manœuvres, and I look forward to facing them with the enemy. It may be that plastic or heavier devons are really more suitable for such streams, or again the rag fellows may repay a try (Chapter VII). Unflattering experience has taught me that the big fish are the reward of those able to steady bait or fly in rapid water. Once the river shapes after the initial days of the coldest spring, our bigger fish tend to push into the heads of streams, as near as they can get to the protection of the rocks that create the barrier. There they are more disposed to take a substantial bait or fly that is held steadily before them than one that skims about and is less easy to see.

Denis has the reputation of getting most of his bag on the bait, but this is largely due to the restriction that his lot is to fish water that has already been well thrashed or is unsuitable for fly. During 1945 he used fly for preference when it was killing, but the instant it flagged he would swing over. On our memorable April 5th, 1945, the four of us had eleven before (a very late) lunch. Immediately after it we got another on the fly, and the three of us stuck to it and captured no more. But Denis had spotted the change and he landed another two on a large prawn.

The fly matters so much to me that instead of discussing it here I have given it its own chapters later on. If there is much water to cover I generally take out both a fly and bait-rod and fish them in turns. There are so often salmon who will fancy the one and spurn the other. Although fishing alone it means more to carry, the change is restful. I find, though, that once I have killed on one or the other that I develop such a bias that I tend to fish the last lucky one all the time. I do not focus adequately on the other, which is, of course, a distressing limitation.

Although we did not disdain prawns (to do so on the day that suits them is idiotic), we only fish them when, after a reasonable trial, we find that they kill. That they do not always is borne out by figures during these two seasons, when we gave them a fair trial :

1945.—*Prawn or shrimp* 20, *spinning baits* 20, *worm* 42, *flies* 97.

1946.—*Prawn* 1, *spinning baits* 24, *worm* 44, *flies* 75.

That worms did comparatively better in 1946 was because of high water the latter end of May and June. I have not yet discovered how to recognize the early spring day when it pays to spin a large prawn. Sometimes in a cold north wind and bright sun they may save a blank day, sometimes when the river is lower in the evening. On the whole I would put my money on rain, wind and rising water. Later in the season, when the shrimp replaces it, swimming and unvaned, it is even more difficult to decide the conditions when it will attract or repel.

The worm is a much less uncertain factor, though he, too, has his off days. It is the worm which introduces Denis at his superlative. Curiously few of our visitors have seriously bothered to learn from him. They loathe it, or they think they understand it already. They may in other rivers. That I have not even tried to handle the art myself is partly due to an abhorrence of eels, partly because as a rule we have had enough wormers. This argument, alas ! is no longer valid in June, so I fear I shall have to reform and practice what I try to preach. Denis once again uses extremely little lead—just enough wrapped round the cast, or hanging from it in little threads (that break off if they meet trouble) to carry the gob out. The cast is made fairly cross-stream and a rod of ten feet is suitable. With one too short there is less control, and it is more difficult to keep the worm off the bottom. The worms do not trundle along the bottom ; they swim clear of it, unless impeded by weed or rock. Lost baits are usually due to the officiousness of eels, who run off with the worms and twist the line round stones. At the end of the swim and before lifting the worm out of the water, pause to make sure that the salmon is not nosing it, as this is a critical moment. You have to be very cute always to recognize an eel from a salmon, and it is not worth running the risk of losing a fish in order to save the bait. Except when he wants to carry the worm well downstream, Denis seldom uses a float ; if he does do so he slits a couple of corks longways and slips them on to the line above the three-foot trace. Two swivels are used, one about 1 ft. 6 in. above the worm, and the other where the trace joins the line. We use nothing but nylon, about three-fifths strength, and buy our hooks unmounted. We find it much more limber in the water than the most pliable wire ; and s.w. gut or the Jap substitute both deteriorate rapidly under the acidity of the worms. Nylon, however, is extremely tricky to mount on the single hook, which needs to be well roughened. This is where I join the team. I hang out flags that out of 100 fish, played on worms or shrimp single hooks in two years, my mounting never betrayed Denis, but I learnt my lesson when I cost Charles the fish we needed in 1945 to make 180. Moist fingers from summer heat and carelessness in not using the more viscous wax gave pride a nasty fall. I now use picture varnish instead of wax, then durofix. It shows how well nylon stands up to the worm acid, that Denis landed ten consecutive fish on the same hook mount.

Mucky water worming needs heavier lead and a much bigger gob. I have not yet succeeded in getting Denis to try the type of mount which theoretically should be so efficient—two hooks, one at each end of a length of nylon, turn back the length so that the slightly smaller hook is situated above the bigger one and loop the doubled nylon above them both. Loops are not the strongest part of the cast, but if one uses the blood-bight and tough nylon one can feel care-free. The old dodge of using a bit of weak old gut to the lead should also save the eel menace, always bad at flood-time. To give line helpfully after the first mumble is not as easy as it sounds—yield too much and the line may belly in the stream and exert a pull; too little may jerk the gob away before the fish can carry it to the hide. My son raises his rod-point and slinks downstream, easing the line as he goes. But it is in judging between give and take that marks the good man, or the good woman like my friend Meg.

In flood, when there is no visibility, in sunshine where there is too much, in the evening while some light exists, there is no time when this method of fishing cannot be used to sweeten the bag. Those who do not like it urge that even if it does not put fish down, it extracts the fellow that they might have caught on a fly to-morrow. There is no proof of this. The bottom feeder is rarely a good riser and to forbid the worm would be a self-denying ordinance which few owners dependent on a reasonable average could afford. While we are getting them on the fly we think it poor policy to worm, and we never do so before lunch. I have, however, no doubt at all that its scaring powers, if any, are too trifling to count. With prawns there will never be a unanimous opinion, but, speaking purely as a fishmonger, I have no objection to spun prawns—or any other bait in the heavy cold waters of spring ; neither do I think that when the prawn or shrimp is being taken that it frightens fish. It is when the fish are off the prawn or shrimp that its use seems to me harmful. I drove along down the Slaney one May and watched its waters being lathered by shrimpers. I had no complaint. The fish that were so obviously off them would be all the more likely to move up to the repose of our beat.

It has always been a regret to me that none of our party has been enterprising enough to alternate the worm with a fresh minnow fished in the same way as the worm. No artificial can rival the natural on warmer days where scent is needed to add to the charm. I hope next year someone will try it on a single hook, wobbling with two small hooks, or spun on an uptrace vane. The fresh loach (collie) is a traditionally good bait here—but first catch your collie, the creatures are hard to come by.

Reflecting over these two years, I ask myself how much more we know about the best weather. One may be judging on a day with no taking fish up. I can only twist the question by saying that heavy rain overhead is always bad ; when it falls we may get a break—this is often the case after the first relieving thunder-shower. On a cold day the brightest sun is a help ; it is not a help on a hot day. A drop in air temperature is excellent in the summer. I doubt if even extreme cold matters in the spring if really fresh fish are up, but it does prevent their moving and coming up. Sometimes we found a cold day blank until an even colder evening followed it. Always I hate floating soapsuds, or a strong upstream wind.

Were I only to be allowed one hour to fish out of the twenty-four I would chose around sunset. If a second choice were permitted I would go for midday (God's). Admittedly bumper bags are generally determined by the morning, but during the past two years we have had to record many more blank mornings than evenings. This is a kindly compensation for those who can only get a short spell on the river after work. I doubt that early morning is so good.

My friend, Sinbad, has since successfully challenged this theory, by rising before dawn and getting two on a worm as the sun touched the water. I fear his achievement will not provoke either Denis or me to reprisals. Our own time rhythm becomes our years and temperament.

Staying out as late as we do, we also wonder how much

the moon—the unclouded moon—puts fish down. I am deeply suspicious of its influence. It sheds an uncanny beam over the face of the waters, and—certainly when it is behind me—I go home. I may be quite wrong and should be more than reassured if my prejudices were to be over-ridden and I could scorn its malice and o'er leap it like the cow.

At the beginning of the season nothing is more difficult than to say whether fish are in the stands or not. They may not show and the water may not be low enough to give one a view. Where underwater cover is scanty one may be able to scour around with polarized glasses, but in rocky places or with undercut banks direct evidence is not obtainable. Later the proof is definitely in the eating. If good fishing during a week of reasonable weather fails to get results, we may say that they have not reached us or have run through our water. Up to the middle of April small single runners may push up on their own without any unusual incentive and be found this afternoon or to-morrow, where there were none this morning or to-day. Such runners are unlikely to pass up to untenanted waters—or to sit down where there are no other fish. The peculiarities of the run have a separate heading later; it is enough to suggest here that on a section of the river where fish are already lying there is always a better chance of meeting some small fresh ones than in an equally good place that has been holding poorly up to date. From May on, even small fresh fish do not appear to come up far without fresh incentive; if there is nothing in a pool to-day, there probably won't be any to-morrow unless the water has risen.

Denis has an instinct for knowing if there is a fish in a particular stand. Again and again we have mocked his optimism, only to be made look silly. In case I have painted too glowing a view of his omnipotence, I hasten to add that there have been days, perhaps several days, of failure even with fish showing and conditions according to plan. Moreover, he doesn't like it a bit! Such chastening is the lot of the salmon-hunter ; it creates that humility that chastens the soul and contributes to the spirit of wonder and thankfulness when things go right.

The compliment that mediocrity pays to its superiors is the belief that they use something special. Dark rumours circulate among the professionals in Newtownbarry as to what Denis " puts up." Were I to whisper " a mouse " all the traps would be cheesed in March. The same suspicions have been bruited about Mr. Pashley on the Wye. Mr. Hutton tells me that the only extra he uses is care—care to change size and depth wherever it is necessary, care over every detail of his set-up. He rarely gets broken in a fish. Moreover, he has that unshakable morale to which I have already tried to do justice, and he abhors leverage.

CHAPTER V

FISHING THE FLY

ON the Slaney the fly dominates our bag. Our stock is not of the permanent character that frequent some rivers ; our fish travel, sit down awhile and respond to appropriate temptation. If water fails, so do they ; when it favours us we get a free take, and if we rarely claim bumper days, at least we have delightful variety of conditions and scope for experiment, even in what looks like very thin water. It is therefore important to make the most of favourable opportunities as they arise before the upward urge removes our stock to those awaiting it above us. That some seasons they do not hurry off upstream has been one of our mysteries.

During the best week we ever had (from April 4th, 1945) we took forty-one, of which thirty were on the fly. It was ideal water for spinning, but three out of four of us were faithful to the greased line, sometimes fishing flies of No. 1 and over. That, I know, would not be an impressive total on many rivers, and I mention it in order to show that at all times we have to work hard for our living. They are not sitting there for the asking. Only during the high cold water of early spring, or in the acid or dead low conditions of later April and May, does the bait or worm definitely replace the charm of the fly. Sometimes when I read of the heavy stocks elsewhere I feel that the little Slaney has so much less to offer, and then I remember the character of its flow and the scope it can give to those who care more for the problem than for the capture.

For some time I had noted, perhaps with puzzled mild disapproval, how effective are Denis's unorthodox ways with a greased line. He casts much as one would with a sunk line—straight and at the traditional 45°—and he goes down steadily, only deflecting his arc when special circumstances decree a change. He invariably catches bigger fish than I do and he also beats most of our guests. Possibly because his aged heavy line holds the fly more firmly at the heads of streams. I know no one who can so securely clip his fly into the very neck of the stream, or make it search the deadly yard of glide above it, where any slip of timing must create the nastiest type of drag. He never wades, and thus misses the strong tactical advantage which the variety of angle and a shorter line gives. For rough waters he prefers a heavy iron, a body dressed with silk or tinsel, and a fairly full hackle—but not too coarse. He also likes a graceful tapered wing. Give Denis a fly he fancies and a salmon he knows and the encounter is likely to be exciting. I am not now alluding to really low conditions, but to the type of day when the rest of us have put up, say, No. 6 low water.

Neither do I claim that we, using lighter stuff, will never catch as much or more than he does. We often do, but without hesitation I can say that his methods mean the end of many salmon, large salmon, that we others (with light lines and skinny dressings) would fail to attract. Because this part of the Slaney appears to suit this particular break with orthodoxy is no reason why the same attack should succeed elsewhere. Dick Harris on the Moy successfully follows Wood or Crossley far more closely. The K.C. fishing above us is also more downstream than most people, but he fishes finer than Denis and prefers to wade. Especially at low water he will use, and kill, with the fly when Denis has taken out his worm outfit.

Among the more elect the cult of size, or lack of size, has become the hallmark of aristocracy. What can be more *distingué* than to hold out a finger-nail upon which reposes a dainty self-conscious No. 12, dressed with half a whisker and a glint of light ? Admittedly there are days when such alone will be fancied ; I myself take pride in the insecticidal art that puts them in my fly-box. The corrective, surely is not to discard the exceedingly minute, but to be ready to step up for a change ? The fact that Denis never fishes the insect standard is probably due to his coarser outfit, but more, I fancy, to the engrossing profit of May worming. Now that our friend Miles Furber has given him one of his own sensitive home-made greenheart rods, we may yet find him outclassing the toothcombers.

In those soul-destroying tables of size the stepping up is immaculately graded. One whisker gives place to two on a hook exactly one size longer than what is known as the day's " standard." If you know a fish is there, and if you have tactfully offered him No. 12 twice, I would suggest give him a rest until he kicks again, change to a stouter cast, make sure you are so well above him that not a tweak of gut will show and, if the water is low and slow, put down a No. 6. If, however, there is a pleasant break, go the whole hog and try a lightly-dressed No. 2. During those two seasons the dramatic success of flies of different size on the same day was outstanding. Previously with air at about 55° F. and water at 50° F. I never took out anything larger than a No. 6 ; now my box will also include a No. 1 or 2 and, in case there comes a sudden interest in naturals, something as small as No. 10, not necessarily lightly dressed. I use conventional size numbers in order to give an idea of the approximate size ; actually the form of dressing may be more important than its size, a subject for consideration when we discuss actual fly-dressing.

Pace and activity are the qualities which an artist will impart, be he drunk or sober. They are the gifts that the rest of us can only master (somewhat) by hard work and a good deal of cheek. In achieving the necessary experience we must beware the false clues that may result from a judgment based on a hopeless day, with fish scarce or sullen (say, rain overhead). The day from which one can best learn is the one when fish are there, but are unaccountably difficult. That is the day to think things out ; if light or other circumstances have changed we may repeat a previous experiment, or try a new one. On the really dud day I withdraw to my cabin and make up gear. Not until sundown do I pick up my old Leonard and try a No. 1 Silver Dr., leaving the dead flat where I marked a rise, until I can only sense my cast as it touches the water.

In our quest to gauge the right pace we should do well to remember that only in moments of wild frenzy will any fish move an inch further than he has to. In a strong stream he is specially reluctant to take much out of himself. One can only try to get well above and " hang the fly." Dick Harris explained to me how, wading at the head of such a stream, he has dibbled in his fly, held out on about a yard of line above the cast, with point high he lets the fly alone just touch the water and holds it firmly as he can. Sometimes the salmon charges at it and breaks the water, then he strikes on sight. If he waits for a pull it is too late. It must be snatch and hold together. It sounds nerve-racking, and as I rarely wade I shall have to try perching myself above and over ; but so sited, I can only command a limited range.

In slow water clearly one must use the bag of the line to give the needed increase of pace. The K.C. mends downstream to hurry things on. I find that my best attempts at achieving exhibitionism are won by drawing in fairly fast by hand. On a flat, with a wind, this works quite nicely. The K.C.'s speciality is the ledge above a weir ; wading with a short downstream line, he lets his fly float down and he tightens the instant he senses the pull, but not till the contact has begun. Naturally he does not get the scissors, but his neat double hook has ended up in the front of many jaws.

Our river is too shallow and snaggy for us normally to chance a dropper, but the 1947 floods encouraged audacity, and now I find myself a convert where such an addition would not introduce too wracking an anxiety. It is not a question of just "doubling the odds"; I do not believe it does so, but the two flies, worked slightly cross-stream, hold their place in a strong current, yet agitate their fibres. Perhaps in pulling against each other they produce a peculiar and varied tension; on a flat they display an inconsequent gaiety, as though they were being blown, not dragged. This applies to greased-line presentation of large flies as well as to the true low-water types. A fairly fully-dressed dropper, such as a deer's tail wing or "shrimp," assists shock tactics. There are days, especially in a wind, when fish seem to need assault. After all, a skilled lady-killer would not choose the same guiles to overcome the Sabine maiden as he would for the Miss Austen heroine. Possibly the accident that my own two heaviest fish this season were Sabines has prejudiced my judgment. As an extra bonus with two flies one tends to form fewer wind-knots. For the dropper knot safest with nylon, see p. 127. When playing a fish on the dropper fly one reminds oneself how rarely even two loose flies cause trouble with a trout; there is the further comfort that the loose end generally lies closely to the salmon's side. One feels that in an emergency there is at least as good a chance of foul hooking him with the tail-fly as of fouling a foreign body !

Don't cast beyond your station applies not only to the mediocre but equally to the long caster. Except on wide unwadable stretches, where a lie cannot otherwise be explored, a short line is, within its scope, more deadly. On a narrow river with a rough spinal current it is impossible to fish the slack beyond the rough water; the attempt only leads to the fly scuttering about and missing the likely spot on one's own side. I had paid lip-service to this comforting reflection before I really quite understood its truth, and stopped trying to get out more than I could handle. A parson friend taught me how to work a very short line by fishing it across, or at only a slight down-angle. Once the line is on the water, swing over the rod and hold the point downstream. The fly will race under the surface without drag, and one will soon realize the best manœuvre to control the pace by rising the rod point or pulling by hand. The journey must be fished out until the bank is reached, as the quickly-travelling fly is often followed and is snatched as it turns and stops. This presentation is an alternative to the normal and is more suitable for a quick, smooth flow than for rough streams or dead flats.

All these types of manœuvres add enormously to the joy of fishing, and I delight in watching others carry them out where my adroitness lags. But the fish must be there and willing to co-operate. Mr. Wood has been made so much of an arch-priest by his followers that we tend to forget that he himself was once an arch-rebel, a shatterer of tradition. To carry on his spirit we should be prepared, like him, to knock down skittles. During the years when I ritualistically bowed the knee to Cairnton I let my fly behave as much like a dead leaf as I could. Now I try to use the stream to make the fly dynamic, always remembering to have lots of line free for rise or pull. It is not enough to do nothing ; one must yield. I pretend I am fishing a worm—or at least half a worm, and let him take it down.

The greased line and the slow strike have brought a revolution, and the former has greatly helped us to use lighter gear—but I don't like abnormally short rods for bank fishing. I always grease because I have only one rod, and I don't care to strain it by recovering soggy line. Instead of using heavy sunk flies, I prefer a bait in the spring. But it is often wise to remove grease and fish deeper late in the year ; with the air oppressive, fish tend to drop to the cooler depths. In *About Fishing* Captain Hartman tells of the rainless summer's day when (admirably prompted by another butler, such as Denis) he watched Opposite Number, fish down, draw blank, and walk away. The butler said it was no matter, the man had been fishing too small. He looked at Captain Hartman's fly-book and chose an 8° Jock Scot, which at once landed them a 22-pounder. The pool was very deep and the water low down in it must have been much cooler. The other dodge of a small fly on a weighted cast might be worth a trial in less dramatic circumstances.

Conversely, clouds and a north wind may create a sudden drop in air temperature which will widen the difference in temperature between it and the water. The colder upper layer will now offer more of the welcome oxygen, and a near surface fly will often be taken freely. Nothing can be more rewarding than such unexpected harvests on a July or August day, and to record these varieties of condition will help us to recognize other such opportunities when they reappear.

Excessive grease in the heat of summer can be washed off with soap—also a useful and portable form of disinfectant. It is well not to grease until one is ready to fish, as line flapping against one's rod is bound to leave some surplus grease upon it. It takes little trouble to solidify grease when the weather heats up and softens it ; get some good wax candle or a bit of paraffin wax and melt it down with your grease, and you will have far less difficulty in getting the line to float.

Although in theory one believes in perfect balance for every type of cast and line, in practice it would be a nuisance, especially for those of us who fish alone, carrying one small pocketful of gear. We may have several thicknesses of cast, but if they are of too wide a range they will not accord with the weight of our line. To become too meticulous is to develop into a bore ; it means a loss in carefree enjoyment of what is not a laboratory exercise, but a sport for ease of mind. Unconvention in technique means little if zest in the hunt is never relaxed.

Our party has long since decided that it is immaterial whether or not one sees the rise. The theory that it is wrong to see it fishing " wet " and right to see it fishing floating is probably bosh. What we see of the rise is much less important than what the fish sees of our fly. In this connection I talked to an eminent oculist, and he told me that little research had been done on the particular make-up of a salmon's eyes as distinct from trout and other more or less similar fish. He did not know to what authority we could refer. Since then I have been in correspondence with Dr. A. G. Huntsman, who is in charge of the research work of the Atlantic Fisheries for Canada. He tells me that one of his workers has taken up this special subject, and his findings may provide us with exciting data. There is considerable evidence to suggest that a salmon's eye reacts more slowly to a sudden change of light than does that of a trout. In other words, a change slightly blinds him. He not only detests strong sun, but he also moves away from the invasion of a dark shadow. He sees worse than a trout does at night, and (this is also a suggestion of Dr. Huntsman) it may be found that his sight is also influenced by a change in temperature. Trout have an exceptionally favourable store of visual purple behind the eye, enabling them to see at night.

There is no evidence, given equal conditions of visibility, that a trout will see a small fly better in the summer, although more small flies are likely to be present then. There is, however, abundant justification for holding that in warm conditions a salmon will see a very small fly or bait better in warm water than it will in cold. It is not only a matter of being fresh up from the sea, because a grilse will behave in the same way as a fish that has been up some time.

Salmon and trout both have a vision of twelve rods to one cone, and recognize movement before detail. Once aroused they turn, face the object with one eye, and use the defined cone vision for discrimination.

To this day we do not know with any certainty whether either salmon or trout can recognize the colours of the spectrum as we see them ; still less do we know whether— if differentiated—special colours attract or repel. Tone is another matter. Practical experience would seem to suggest

(I find myself alleging like a lawyer) that pike and bream may like red, but can we cross ourselves and declare we *know* that the same applies to salmon and trout ? We may fancy so ; I do myself. I have the comforting corroboration of Mr. Hutton, who says he finds red and gold excellent in both bait and fly when fish are getting choosey. Claret, another form of red, has a long, late season tradition. One has only to pick up Major Hales' book on tying standard salmon flies or look at Halford's list of dry-fly dressings for trout to realize what a simplification has occurred in the past twenty years. We are left with the present-day substitutes of flash, sparkle, the opaque, the translucent, and, still more latterly, in both trout and salmon fly dressing, the essential factor of activity.

How does this quality of liveliness apply to what we know of the salmon or trout's eye ? Amidst so much uncertainty a few known facts stick out. Fish do not possess stereoscopic vision ; but neither does any animal below the status of a monkey, except to an elementary extent. A dog's eyes are better sited than are those of a fish for seeing in front, but watch him chase a chicken, running on view. How easily he over-distances himself, his head a bit on one side to assist a single view from one eye. A fish lying with its head upstream has a far more obstructed field of vision. It is never convincing to argue back from ourselves, but try shutting one eye and placing a finger longways midway across the other, about an inch away. You have now, so I have been told, a fair approximation of a fish's field of vision—two fields. How different is this to the neat little cone we have been apt to revere in the diagrams, where the fish is shown lying like a decanter, waiting to be filled at its head through a funnel. Obviously it can see in front and it can see above, but it requires extra stimulation to notice an object. In its migrations it is known to rely more upon messages to its lateral line than upon sight to guide its course. In feeding it has the further aid of smell. Therefore, it has not to depend upon sight alone to warn it of coming danger, or of the promise of approaching food. Undoubtedly sight is a valuable auxiliary in helping it to detect danger and select diet. From experiments with the reflex actions of frogs it has been learnt that movement supplies just this stimulation to notice, especially the quick movement of an object in flight. The implications of this upon our view of a fish in a stream are many.

Placed as it is, more or less like a flat button at the side of the head (we are not here alluding to flounders), the fish's eye cannot be ideally sited for looking above ; nor is it best suited for upstream observation. He must see better at the side ; but there his vision becomes more obviously monocular. Mr. Arthur Hill tells me he has spent hours on a bridge watching fish rise. He never saw one take straight upstream. They all turned. As far as I can remember, because the subject has only recently begun to interest me, most of the trout I have seen move to my dry-fly have come sideways. They will follow it after a turn ; or they wait for it and then rise ; they don't move upstream to meet the fly above where we have marked them rise before.

The theory that a fly or bait is better seen if presented sideways to the stream is useful, because it offers variety and change, but it is doubtful whether it is intrinsically better than a downstream presentation, when the bait or fly tends to be viewed in profile by the fish from the side. How often do we get a surprise last pull when fly or bait is being recovered upstream ? We all know how fatally we have been let down by neglecting due allowance for this postscript snatch. It would be foolish indeed to claim that any one angle of presentation must be better than another, but the fact that I personally meet more fish when casting generally at an angle of 45 degrees than I did when casting across stream, cannot fail to impress me personally. Actually a straighter line tends to give the life we have been discussing, and this probably is more important than the angle of travel. To be aware of that button of an eye may help to explain certain errors in synchronization in a salmon. Mouth and eye (like our hand and eye) don't always work together. Sometimes a river fishes better from one bank than the other ; sometimes a fish comes in unsuspectingly to the gaff until a turn of the head makes him notice us and sends him tearing off. It certainly suggests that the more we try a different approach, the more likely we shall be to demonstrate our attraction in one or other of the two fields of sight.

The dry-fly man, who is in a much better position to make accurate observations of the rise, should be able to help us. Does a rising trout appear at the one time to be more interested in one side than the other ? Does the position of the sun affect a favoured side ?

Among the many factors that make up vision that of refraction, due to the bending of light at the water's surface, has often been graphically described. It is a measurable phenomenon and to the human eye and brain a double image would be viewed. Until we know more of the salmon's automatic adjustment, if any, to this natural delusion, it would be rash to base any special technique upon it. The reactions involve the uncertainties of mind and instinct as well as the certainties of measurement. It might be tempting to suggest that a trout, whose diet depends upon locating minute surface objects, would counter such a delusion more readily than would a salmon, returning from the deep sea. Yet what evidence have we that fresh salmon differ in vision from kelts that have spent more than a year in fresh water ? Why should we assume that the returned emigrant has forgotten his gluttonous child life when he had to reckon with direct vision, refraction, reflexion, and the rest ? Not only Dr. Freud, but experienced Jesuits alike stress the retention of early habits and fixations. In our present semi-ignorance we are likely to learn more by patient trial and error, many errors, than by too easy assumptions.

CHAPTER VI

THE FLY IN THE VICE

WHETHER we buy or dress our own, the fly is born of original vice, or of fingers that act as vice. Its history ranges from the simplest to the most complicated gradations of colour and glory, to translucency, stream-line, and monotone. We are at present engulfed in the dynamic zone of activity. Feathers are being supplemented by furs and the deer's tail wing is wagging strongly.

The term, " deer's tail wing," is flauntingly unbiological. Originally the salmon " fly " wing was intended not only to convey the essential form of flight, it was also expected to exert esoteric appeal ; its dressing was the crowning feat of the craftsman. Strips of brilliant colour, cheeks of jungle-cock, and foundations of peacock herl were ritual-istically associated with their correct standard types, and —looking into the window of a tackle shop—who can say that even now they are outmoded ? Most of us will agree that colour, as attraction, has been over-stressed, and re-cently our purists have compensated for the loss of one complication by replacing it by another. There arrived, about ten years ago, a reverence for form and tone that would not have been out of place in an art school. Mallard had to be dark with ivory roots, wings and dubbing for a Lemon Grey needed an unnerving subtlety of selection ; even the Blue Charm might not expose its strands of teal but was required to overlay them with a modest " veil " of mallard.

Following these refinements there came, still more re-cently, the stark school of dead plain for visibility. Rich yellow or unrelieved black wings elbowed out the standard types, their dressers voicing the claim that they could be fished on hooks a size smaller than those used with broken tones. In brown coloured water yellow-orange shows up splendidly ; it also appears to attract in sunlight and I, for one, never feel confident nowadays that I have fully explored a stand until I have put over a plain yellow or a black type. Of course if I feel like it, I try a mottled change, too. With the exploitation of the unbroken coloured wing the factor of livelier action began, but quill feathers, even when dressed in the Kilroy manner—laterally between the rounds of the throat hackles—did not look particularly appealing in a monotone. Other materials were sought. Dyed raffia in small strips is disappointing —when soaked it becomes limp ; silk worm gut, associated with Baden-Powell, is useful, but the goat's beard—familiar in the early Studleys—has had a better innings. Dyed a rich yellow and shaped like a straight shaving brush, it kicks in the water. When first introduced the fly was hampered by unnecessary furbelows on the body. Several joints, broken by black herl, bits of chatterer and tinsel were involved in the prescription and the resultant product was apt to fray under the toothy embrace of a kelt. Admittedly one could attach a goat's beard to a plain hackled body, but the fibres were straight and even, and hardly seemed worth all the trouble of stranding. While golden pheasant toppings could be had, their curve, colour, and durability gave us the animation we fancied. During the war this type of pheasant supply diminished and the feather alternative of dyed swan, though adequate in small sizes, proved frailer and a bit bolstery in a heavy wing.

Many of us first heard of the deer's tail in winged form through a book from the U.S.A. It described how a resourceful Guide, having lost his gear, tied up an emergency fly from a single white tuft (snipped off the tail of the quarry destined for the camp supper). So successful was the tuft that its successors, dyed, became embodied, or rather winged, on the Studleys and other types of many professional and amateur dressers. Unlike the long hairs from Billy (which are wound round a card, tied in the middle, and then doubled back after the initial tie on the neck of the hook), the hairs from the deer's tail are cut off in a tuft, held firmly, and tied on to expose their natural curve. The separate hairs have a slight springy curl and a definite taper. Undoubtedly a wing so composed is more skittish than is one derived from either goat or feather. Owing to their inelasticity, hairs are not easy to tie in securely, and many dressers turn back the ends, which make a head ; but I have not found this necessary for salmon.

As soon as I saw such a fly in action, I voiced my plaint in the right quarters and was rewarded by the gift of four scuts from fallow deer. I removed the black hairs from a pair of them and dipped the white residue in rich daffodil dye (3d. from the chemist) and fixed the tone in an alum bath. Dried, they looked like two shapely pheasant crests. I kept a fat allowance for myself, and shared out the balance (on the bone). There were still a pair left. These I decided to leave *au naturel* in order to try plain back and white· wings. To anyone who believes in black unadorned, nothing could be more tempting. My faithful Black Maria deserted her wisp of inky quill in favour of the dear gazelle (Maria's body is silk, half yellow, half black, and she has a black hackle-throat, and nothing else whatsoever) ; with her new permed wing she was clearly out for trouble. The same type of black tuft makes the Bloody Butcher even bloodier. The pure white wing I have attached to an un-garnished black silk body relieved only by red tail, hackle, and throat. One is so much accustomed to placing light tones below and dark above that the reversal seems rather shocking, but I hope it may simulate something *in extremis* —tummy top-side.

Let it not be imagined that if you cut off your tuft and tie it on, it will at once give you stream-line. It can be the very devil. My first shot was a cross between Shockheaded Peter and Medusa. I assured the scandalized Denis that it was meant to look like that in the highest circles. When he had moved off I took it to pieces and tried again. To combine individuality with sound team spirit—and a touch of stream-line, it is necessary to cheat. First twirl and pinch the tuft until it looks right, lay it on a longer neck than you usually allow, tie in, taper the head, finish off with Cellire. Now, hold the wing by its middle, assuring its nicest " set," take the Cellire and apply it to the spring of the shoulder ; do not relinquish it till secure. Extra long fibres can be snipped off. There are other more orthodox ways of curbing exuberance, if you want to do so—many people don't—but I recommend Cellire every time. You will not interfere with the active lower half, but you will secure a pleasant arch and a neat entry into the water.

After further experience of fishing fur wings, I have noticed that they can give two distinct forms of activity, longwise or lateral. The doped wing, as just described, slips neatly into the water and swings in addition to fanning. It is less disposed to " flair " in the wrong place than is one tied on in an untapered bunch. The bunchy type (better known in the U.S.A. as the " Patent ") appeals by its untapered, fanlike action. There is no stream-line about it ; it is held in a strong current on a short line, where it spreads and closes like a V in the water. On our river we have hardly the turbulent conditions to do it justice, but its hybrid, like a restrained shaving brush, has proved to be not only conspicuous but attractive, when shock tactics are required, especially in a wind.

Following the further quest for activity, I have lately been introduced to the mohair wing—fine, pliable, silky mohair. Instead of fan action there is swerve ; the fibres do not work independently, they cleave together and end in a very fine taper. The wing, extending well beyond the hook, wriggles like a little golden eel in a clear stream. It kills in much lower water than would the same size of

shaving brush type. There is no question that the natural
curl of mohair imparts more life than would a golden
pheasant crest ; it looks gay and irresponsible in the water.
A body of silver tinsel, and a throat of blue show up the
golden quality of the wing. Being finer, mohair can be
tied in more neatly than the deer's tail, and it is easier to
handle in small sizes. I possess a hank of blue-black
mohair, which I shall try out with a silver body in the
evening. To claim that any one fly is better than another
is to court ridicule, but the type that is based on action
may help to narrow the margin between the good man,
who imparts it naturally, and the medium fisher, who
struggles to achieve it.

My friend the K.C., and several of our party, have had
excellent results in very low water with the shrimp fly.
Personally I am uninterested in the exact feathers used.
The point to aim at is the type of tail and of hackle which
will kick. Several good R.I. fibres, or of pheasant tail,
for whisk, butted by a turn or two of badger hackle, a
pair of prickly little galena feathers as midway wings, and
an R.I. hackle throat, deftly put together on a No. 6 to
No. 10 L.W. hook will give all the range needed. I use a
half yellow, half black jointed silk body, with a thread of
silver tinsel for luck—but only for luck, as the tandem
hackle and long tail is all that really matters. I know the
conventional tie includes Amhurst pheasant and jungle-
cock, but, although I happen to own two bursting bosoms
of jungle-cock, I only use them for barter. I don't like
their texture, and their enamel seems to me crude. In
this my opinion differs both from Denis and, perhaps more
impressively, from Mr. Hutton, and I do tie up Thunders
for Denis flanked with jungle-cock, but not for myself. My
prickly galena tips give me the break I need in the shrimp
wing. I have also tied up this type in shell-pink and have
killed ; possibly it might be better than the other on a
really natural shrimp day, but who knows ? For the
coming season, we hope to experiment more with the fluent

tandem type of hackle. Black Maria, who, in 1945-46, increased her reputation as *femme fatale*, is to be deprived of all wing and become a débutante nymph.

In stressing activity so much, I remember the amusement it caused us long ago when old Peter Murphy, the gardener, would tell my husband that he would fulfil a request "with the greatest animosity." Later we learned from a philologist that the original meaning came from *animus*. Peter was a grand hand with a trout rod : I like to think him now, on a farther shore, presenting his Hare's Ear with the greatest of animosity.

Glint or flash is a quality that may be happily combined with action. Curiously enough, in bait fishing gold is as popular as silver—witness the popularity of the golden sprat—but in flies silver is used more. It may only be the force of habit, or because gold tinsel is more expensive, but the fact that yellow or orange feathers (or fur) can be so easily added to replace the quality of gold may account for the difference. White feathers cannot make up for the glint of silver, which shows up in opaque or milky water and, Mr. Hutton tells me, is particularly suited to flood conditions on the Wye. In the brown flow of the Slaney an orange or yellow wing is our first choice, because we believe it to be more conspicuous. In clear water our record of catches on the Silver Dr. (tied with the fewest elements and an opaque wing) make it our inevitable favourite in the evening. Yet there are certain stands where the Silver Dr. (with a more translucent wing) appears to beat all others in the day-time.

Viewed optically and apart from attraction, there must be combinations of tone appropriate for special conditions of lighting. Others may be found to do as well, but if one has the benefit of well founded local experience it is surely worth while to give that choice a trial ? Local legend still persists of the "poison" that used to be dressed by the lamented Martin, "the Goat"; and of titled English visitors unloading gold—or its liquid equivalent—upon the

F

dresser.   It is impossible to prove any of these stories now, but I know that if the Goat's shade were to stand behind my shoulder, point with a finger, and say " try that one," I should (if I had not first died of fright) tie on his choice immediately.

In low summer water and daunting bright sunshine, Charles distinguished himself using a glint of silver body, two herls of peacock wing, and a throat of small chatterer, masking a No. 12 hook.   Whether he was being natural or provocative I do not know ; I only marvelled.   The superstition of blue for spring, claret for autumn has, we think, been blown away.   A variant of red—as in claret—is always good ; while blue makes a nice collaboration of tone at any time.

There remains the deliberate imitation, of which the now popular " Daddy " is the most amusing.   He looks extremely clever and would scare to fits more people than Miss Muffit.   To tie he is simplicity.   He needs some pheasant fibres wound round him for the body. (They are taken from a tail feather.)   The genuine spider has four pairs of legs, but the dresser only gives him three. These also are made of pheasant's brown fibres, knotted in the middle (before being attached) to give an angular bend and " knees."   They are spaced to fit the body and tied in laterally in pairs.   There is nothing else but a hackle. Officially it should be rusty dun, but anything " mousey " will do, even badger.   They can be most effective for salmon tied on, say, a No. 8 L.W. hook, and would, I imagine, tempt the most fastidious trout if presented dry.

Anyone who has watched a trout-man will keep a few March Browns and Greenwells handy.   Miles Furber tells of how, when fishing the Cork Blackwater in May, the colour was so thick that he replaced a No. 1 by a gaudy 2° ; it did no better.   Wearily he moved upstream to find a young lad playing a salmon on a trout rod.   Before Miles could interfere the boy threw down his rod and tugged

the line by hand. The light cast broke at the fly.
" I don't want to waste any more time," he growled ;
" that's the fourth damned nuisance I've hooked to-
day."

When on the subject of size we may all agree that the
time has come for us to be given a dependable standard
of measurement, observed by all retailers here and overseas. Even so, this cannot cover the different styles of
dress we may prefer to give them. Mine vary from hobble
skirt to crinoline. I don't myself like L.W. smaller than
No. 8 (Hardy's gauge), and I think the short-neck can be
overdone. I like the more rounded sea-trout type for
smaller patterns, if they are to be relied on ; but how many
of us bother to do justice to our hooks by keeping them
needle-pointed.

A friend has given me so neat a method of dubbing
either a trout or salmon fly that I offer it with due acknow-
ledgments to its author, a clever angler from Co. Wicklow.
The tying silk is strictly limited to tying-on and the fur is
held by the tinsel. Flat bands cannot be used, so the
imposing standard uniforms, wherein a pompous broad strip
is followed by an " A.D.C." just behind it, must assume a
more modest Battle Dress, though not necessarily one with
less glint.

The first act is to take the fur (fine rabbit or hare's fluff
becomes a pleasure to handle) and to tease it into quite
small tufts, arranged in a convenient row (Fig. 1 A). The
fibres should not be too long, or they will get in the way of
the tying, and one needs a much lighter dressing than is
at first realized. If two colours are to be mixed, blend
them in advance ; if the body is to be of jointed contrasting
colours, then have them ready, so to speak, on the palette,
as the final operation must be carried through quickly.
Now we take a stiletto (Fig. 1 B), or a long pin, or other
minor lethal weapon, and plunge it firmly into the table.
(If you cherish the surface of the table, borrow the bread-
platter.) For a fly of about 2° size, approximately 6 inches

of tinsel is needed; for a larger fly, flat "oval" tinsel works well, but the thickness of the tinsel should be only half the thickness of that normally selected, because later it will be doubled. It should be very bright. When one is familiar with the amount of material preferred, it is easy

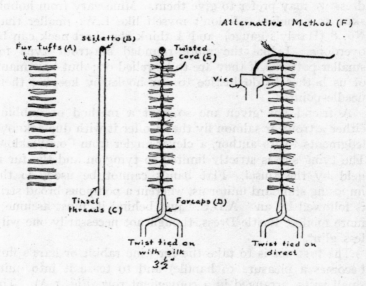

FIG. I.—ONE WAY OF DUBBING

to make a strip long enough to dress several flies, but at the start it is safer to provide for one at a time. The tinsel C is doubled and the middle is held round the impaled pin and the two ends kept close together in tension. They now both receive a liberal dressing of Cellire. Before the Cellire dries, take a dentist's or a philatelist's small tweezers and push in the tufts between the two tinsels. They must be put in evenly and not too thickly. Apart from the benefit of retaining the fur, the varnish helps to preserve the polish of the tinsel, never easy to brighten up on a dubbed body. The tinsel is now gripped in a pair of artery forceps, D, and the two threads are twisted until the fur is tightly wound into a cord (Fig. 1. E). Carry the twist all along or the hold on the fur will be insecure. Leave alone until the varnish is dry. While this is proceeding, put the hook in the vice and attach tag and tail in the usual manner. Tie in a foundation silk of floss. I prefer one of lighter tone to the fur to be used. White goes admirably if a luminous effect is aimed at, or, where gold tinsel is to follow, daffodil yellow helps. Make the silk body as slim or as plump as you want, according as you desire it to sink or search the surface. When this is done, see that the tying silk is back at the tail ready to attach the furry tinsel; once that is in, it returns to the neck of the hook and the tinsel is wound on spirally and fastened in there. I do not use a body hackle, only a throat, as the dubbing is enough. The slightest pricking with a pin will dress the fur fibres and the tinsel will glow underneath.

That is the operation as I was given it. I make the variation of discarding the pin and of using the hook direct which avoids the need to tie in and is much stronger. The plan, they tell me, works grandly for trout flies; indeed, its author devised the dodge for that purpose. I shall not use the old method any more for salmon, as this one gives a more sprightly result.

It has not been my good fortune to fish much for trout recently, but I account it a sad year if I am unable to keep my hand in with a dry-fly for a few summer days each year. I slip into my long boots and flick with my old 8-foot Hardy under the spreading branches and between the weed beds, which preserve the Derry from other visitors. I have a choice of three large loaded boxes of paternal flies. Most of them have atrocious little pinched hooks, but I have selected a few with more menacing gapes, hackled for choice, and provided I can contrive to plant them where needed, I can generally get a rise. But, and this is the strange thing, these little trout are far more cunning and difficult to rise twice than were the sophisticated pounders of the Avon and Coln, at Bibury. You mustn't show a Deiry trout one inch of gut or he'll curl his lip. A hooked cast, like a note of interrogation, just short of him, may get him, but more often a pert smaller fellow lying below will tell tales by scooting upstream and spreading panic. Still, I have had happy times and have provided breakfasts. I hope that new and lovely nylon waders, light as feathers, will appear before I am eighty-five, and so prolong my days. Even since Bibury, in 1916, I have found Wickham, Red Tag, with Tup or Blue Bottle enough ; probably if I fished wet—below the surface film— I should need more, but authority, perhaps instigated by Lord Grey, seems to favour the lowest common denominator of three or four, for dry. All are agreed that the tying matters enormously, but the selection, allowing for changes in size, could be housed in a match-box. Mr. Cass mentions Pheasant Tail, Tup, Blue Upright and Black Gnat, with a readiness to make the first and second alone serve. Others prefer the Fore and Aft (dressed with R.I. Red), or a Lunn's Fancy, Red Spinner or Captain Hartman's any ginger " Antonio." Must we, then, declare that the expert entomologist will no longer reap the exceptional occasional harvest that he has earned by his knowledge ? Certainly not : to do so would be to introduce *always* instead of *usually*. We may believe that this special day will not happen very often and that if we went out prepared for it with the full equipment of the White Knight, we ourselves might not even recognize the One and Only when it hatched.

Probably the large majority of dry-fly fishers will split the difference and continue to dip into their experience and use a wider range. They may not claim to recognize species with the precision of the professional entomologist, but they will have their memories of the day when one only of their selection wrought havoc on the waters, to their own justification and the confounding of their rivals.

The dry May-fly follows his own set technique, ending in the half-mourning of the evening spent gnat. On the Irish lakes he is ousting the " dap " among the *élite*. I imagine that the bass, which rises to the fly more obligingly off the Irish sea-board than elsewhere, is not choosey if offered a white goose-wing ; but of this I write only from second hand.

Even with wet flies, which appear to be less of caricatures of the real thing, and with the sacred Nymph, a very small range will meet the changing seasons (usually). What we call Rails in Ireland (sedges ?) are used for black night work. I believe, however, that the K.C. is right, when he ties his hackles differently for downstream to upstream presentation. Animosity again.

The K.C. has won such renown for sea-trout work in the West that those who want sport there would do well to discover him or his like and learn his patterns. The art of the sea-trout varies with the different localities, even the hours of take. I have landed several on the dry Red Tag, perhaps because I knew so little. There are few fish I respect so much. The same Red Tag brought me success with rudd on an Irish pond, as well as with grayling in England. It is my hope that in my next incarnation I may be privileged to cast for more soft-mouthed fish. It must improve timing. Looking back, I am sure I was too quick—they hadn't time to suck. If I am given a second chance I shall . . . But, instead of rash speculations, let me record a very coarse fish story. A friend, dry-flying in the Slaney, near Tullow, saw a tempting rise. It was latish in the evening and he cast prettily over it. His ginger quill floated nicely over the circling rise, everything was up to instructional film standard, the strike perfectly timed and the rod was bent. Imagine the anti-climax when the admiring beholders on the bridge saw him reel in an 11-inch eel. Mercifully this doesn't happen often.

I have often been asked whether our suggested range of pseudo-standard flies, based on Black Maria, have fulfilled expectations. They have indeed. For pseudo Jock, the yellow-and-black silk body (already Jock-like) affects a fluent teal hackle-throat, and just a black turkey wing, white tipped. For pseudo-Thunder, the yellow silk becomes orange and the hackle ditto, *voilà tout !* However valuable the translucent wing may be in bright conditions, the need for something solid and opaque persists. With long, weighty irons the dubbed body and bolstery wing is just as useful as it was to our grandfathers, in the appropriate place, only the elements to form the pattern can be far simpler. Moreover, the widespread success of the shrimp fly reminds us that even a tail may be more than a useless appendage.

One of the minor nuisances of recent dollar scarcity has been the difficulty in getting fly-tying materials from across the Atlantic, where admittedly the stock vastly exceeds anything that can be offered this side. Among treats ahead, polar bear fur is the most tempting, with its glint, texture, and curl. In golden hue it is a dangerous rival to the stiffer deer's scut. Every sort of fur is now exploited in the States and there nylon has largely replaced silk for tying. A delightful little bobbin is supplied to hold the nylon ; it hangs pendant from the hook, yielding length as one needs it. Some type of viscous dressing would still be needed with nylon tread, and I propose continuing with the picture varnish, which I have come to prefer to wax. Let those who intend to use nylon casts avoid a tadpole head on their flies. Nylon *must* have room above the eye.

It must be some compensation for Britons that their hooks, in every shape and form, are still preferred on the other side of the Atlantic.

CHAPTER VII

BAITS AND BAITING

> " I think you would find at least half a dozen good performers
> with the fly-rod for every really good bait fisherman. Anyone
> can learn to cast a bait, but how many know how to work a
> bait when it is in the water ? Each pool indeed each part of
> a pool, requires different treatment . . . in one catch at
> Hampton Bishop, not 25 yards long, I had to change the
> weight of the leads twice if I wanted to fish the pool properly."

I QUOTE from a letter which Mr. Arthur Hutton wrote
to me. It behoves those of us who prefer to follow
the fly to learn the lesson and with it the humility that
does not always distinguish those of us who prefer to follow
the feathers. Indeed, it was largely owing to the greater
difficulty which I found in fishing other baits that I became
so much attached to the wooden fellows, which by their
nature are able almost to fish themselves, swinging to and
fro and up and down, as the current carries them. This
especially applies to the technique of using very light leads
where such are appropriate.

In cold water coarser inducements are needed ; although
fresh fish may snatch at anything, a bigger object is less
likely to be overlooked. There is, moreover, the factor
of the bait's revolution. I was interested to see that some
tentative suggestions on this subject which I had already
made were borne out by observations of Mr. R. H. Ferry
(writing in the magazine of the Salmon and Trout Association), though he did not apply his remarks directly to bait
revolution. He was writing of the amazing influence of
the lateral line on the behaviour of trout, which he compared with the reactions of Radar. If Radar is so sensitive
that it can enable the receiver to plot the flight of gulls,
is it extravagant to suggest that the commotion induced

by a rapidly revolving bait should have positive reactions on a fish ? Blind fish, he reminds us, can feed themselves by using the messages of vibration, and they can attack other fish. Any movement a fish makes sets up vibrations which echo back from submerged rocks and warns it of their presence, and so collision is averted. Years ago it was believed that the whirr of a spoon was recognized by a mahseer in the snow-fed opaque waters of India more quickly than its flash was seen. Again, in the cold waters of Kashmir we used fly-spoons for the rainbows when they were first introduced by the Maharajah. The spin of the bait then not only affects its steadiness and the depth of its swim, but it *may* attract—or repel. A spoon makes a terrific commotion, probably more so than any other bait and we have found that it attracts correspondingly well in dirty water, especially on a cold, windy day.

The spoon has the disadvantage that it hooks less surely than a devon. We now follow out Mr. Hutton's free flight, attaching limber wire on to which we mount the treble, not to the tail-hole provided, but to the ring at the spoon's head. This plan permits the treble to swing free of the spoon ; the professional make-ups of both spoons and artificials rarely give hooking space ; Mr. Hutton's plan also avoids detestable leverage once the fish is hooked. To prevent the flight playing bumble-puppy during the cast, one can put a turn or two of the finest wire through the tail-hole and round the flight ; this wire will at once give if a fish is hooked. I find the spoon works better in the water if the flight hangs free ; it does not appear to get caught up in the hook.

To those who prefer bought artificials or natural baits it is well to repeat the warning against this bugbear of leverage. The more I examine the position of the hook in the fish's mouth the more am I scared even of a treble. Consider how many more treble hooks break or straighten that we find occurs with single hooks. When to the inevitable leverage exerted by a treble we add the longer and worse fulcrum of a fixed bait attached to it, we court trouble indeed. The devon principle, whereby the bait runs up the line on hooking, is far the safest in artificials ; the shape of the devon itself makes for quick hooking, since the fish's mouth slips off its hard tapered end. Bought devons, as we have noted, often give little room for this easy hooking, and Fig. 3 suggests how the use of a second much smaller bead or a knot of binding can assure the required distance and protect the binding of the hook. Another bogey is the patent attachment often used to slip the devon's swivel on to the trace. Admittedly such devices are quickly adjusted ; a welcome aid with cold fingers and spectacles left at home, but we have noticed that of visiting guests at least half use clips bulky enough to restrain a bulldog. As a result the devon shell cannot run up the line and it creates a fulcrum as long as itself. For naturals what is called the " Jock Scot " type swings free when the fine wire binding the bait gives away. There is, however, always the temptation to overdo the wire binding, which connects the tail of the bait to the mount, especially if the bait has become a bit battered in casting and needs a corset to hold it together. Unless it is really lightly attached the wire cannot break, as intended, when the fish is hooked.

In selecting the type of artificial bait, habit clutches at one's reason ; without falling into adolescent passion for a lovely creature with mascaraed eyelashes, one still expects lateral shading, back dark and tummy lighter ; stream-line is admired ; smoothness is all. Yet revolve this lifelike imitation and note what happens. All lateral markings disappear and the dominant tone will kill the others, producing a muddy, rather ineffective neutral. I no more venture to claim that what I think a well-coloured devon will kill more than a bought one, than I would dare to exalt one fly pattern over another. It is, however, not extravagant to claim that original types of colour scheme will give their author such morale that he will fish them better.

All those whom I have started in this industry of shaping, finishing, and colouring (and I myself was given the initial idea by somebody else) make much more sophisticated jobs than I do. They mould lovely shoulders and sand-paper away the least inequality. They paint fashion-plate bodies, or apply subtle feather effects. I don't say it matters, but I know it cannot help. When I look at them I think I must endure the same kind of emotion that would overcome a follower of Picasso when confronted with the work of Sir John Millais. Except that mine strive for a sound margin of wood at head and tail, they might have been whittled by an intelligent school-boy. Their surface still shows where the knife left it, and the blobs of colour are applied solely with an eye to rotation. As a result the colours look distinct, not confused in the water. I obtain flash by recessing a spiral of gold or silver against a dark background, or by dabs of metal tones applied beltwise, but rarely longwise. Gold is best shaken on in dry powder form with a brush upon a ground of wet cellire. All baits should first be given an undercoat of some common matt paint, in white or cream. It is well to make batches at a time. To dry them I use a spike of wire, on the same principle as they employ in shops for impaling bills ; the painted devons are threaded on to this out of harm's way until dry. It is no use to hurry on the job.

For colours we like plain gold or silver when required to show up ; blobby brown and cream for conditions of better visibility, or, as Mr. Hutton prefers, shabby brown for clear, and dark green touched with gold, or dark green with a flashing spiral for the evening. Next season we hope to try out Mr. Hutton's scarlet and gold. My example looks like the opening of Parliament. It may seem premature to discuss the colouring before one describes how the devon is made, but that affair is simple, if one has the wood and a penknife and has ever looked at a devon.

A length of syringa (*philadelphus*) or of *Deutzia*, well seasoned (the immature stuff has too large a central opening), is so good that it is not worth while to seek another, although the more adventurous may prefer the harder spindle-wood (*euonymous europæus*). Make sure that the hollow is kept central during the whittling. Once the shell is made, pencil in where the vanes (at an angle of 45°) are to sit, and cut out snicks with a fine hacksaw. It is not easy to ensure that the nicks are made exactly opposite to each other, as pencil-marks may not follow the true line. Miles Furber has made it foolproof. He shapes a few inches of lath with a long taper at one end, thus :

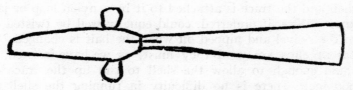

FIG. 2.—WEDGE FOR CENTERING VANES

The point is then stuck into the channel in the devon and the nick cut into the bait's back. To make the exact antipodal cut on the tummy, turn the lath over.

Remember to scoop the channel clean or the fragments left inside will swell and catch the swivel. It is well to have half one's stock spinning in reverse. It is difficult to avoid kink with rapid rotation, and nothing will undo trouble if it does arise, so certainly as reverse spin. The vanes are bedded into the nicks with cellire or durofix, and as they are based on the same medium as the cellire, they become part of the bed.

Early in the war I wanted to secure Cellophane sheeting thinner than that usual in vanes. Hitherto I had been content with scrap derived from old side-screens in motor-cars. Dreading leverage, I like something that will bend in the fish's mouth, or break if it sticks between rocks. Moreover, thin Cellophane is far and away easier to shape with scissors. Boldly I wrote to the secretary of a company that specialized in cellulose paper, and he sent round a representative from another company (I cannot remember the name) ; four shillings passed, and I became enriched with a lifelong supply of one orange and one red sheet of Cellophane, firm enough to make a bait revolve and filling all my other requirements. With a curved nail scissors the sheets can be cut as easily as a playing card.

With a complete painted vaned shell ready (Fig. 3) there now remains the mount. Usually these have to be carefully measured to fit each size of shell, but with our type only two sizes are needed because the swivel lies inside the roomy shell and the trace is attached to it by a nylon loop or jam knot. Wire, if preferred, could equally well be twisted on to the swivel and nipped off when the bait is changed. If patent clips are used they must, as we have insisted, be small enough to allow the shell to run up the trace on hooking. There is no difficulty in running the shell up the trace for mounting. I prefer to have no metal showing above the devon's mouth in low water. With a roomy hollow it is, of course, necessary to use a biggish bead.

Nobody has yet been able to prove conclusively whether tail trebles, doubles, or singles (or possibly tandem singles in reverse) are the most practical for hooking and holding. Doubles or singles every time for a side-arming of a natural —but for the tail. I only wish I knew. Whichever one selects, the plan of the additional small bead or of extra binding will keep the hook away from the devon, even the buffer of the eye of a hook is not always enough to give clearance.

Compared with single hooks, doubles and trebles are refreshingly simple to tie on. To mount them with nylon or gut one binds the tapered hook ; but with wire it is not safe to bind, one must use an eyed hook and twist the wire.

The next operation is to slide on the bead. If you wait until the swivel is on it is too late, and you will weaken the wire untwisting it. The diagram below illustrates the finished article.

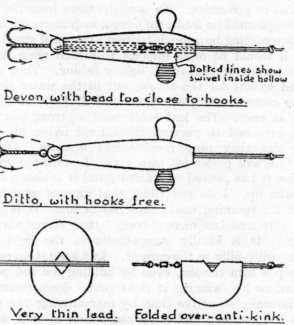

Devon, with bead too close to hooks.

Ditto, with hooks free.

Very thin lead. Folded over-anti-kink.

FIG. 3

With two sizes of hooks and two lengths of mounts you can mount any shell you have, unless your range extends far more widely than any that I have. Naturally you will durofix all bindings.

In regard to the distances between swivels on the trace, every taste will differ. Long nylon lengths mean that economy is not needed. For early spring work we use 3/5 (or stronger) and a blood bight loop. For finer wear the swivel should not be so near the bait; in fact a double one at the top should serve on a 3-ft. or 3-ft. 6-in. trace. Denis likes two leads, and he cuts them out himself out of fine sheet lead. They are painted in blobs of dark green and black. It does not do to make them too conspicuous or attractive. To save the trace from the friction of these pinched on leads, we have a loop above each swivel. It is astonishing how much friction nylon will stand. Using wire, it would be more difficult to attach these flat leads which permit of such much lighter fishing. They give the desired weight for the throw, but in the water they turn in the current and play ducks and drakes. A solid lead sinks at once. The leaf leads need a strong pinch when being attached to prevent them from flying off. Unless quite flat they may revolve like a vane. Obviously, everyone will prefer his own type of outfit ; I give ours because it has proved so efficient, and it is cheap and easy to make up. I do not think that anyone who has used nylon for spinning could fault its action. It is less stiff than wire and has more " bone " than either s.w. gut or " Jap." It is ideally sympathetic to the light devons, tossing willy-nilly in the current. In fishing them remember to keep a firm tension, even by holding the rod point upstream, or by swinging it right round downstream ; they are naturally so active that by manœuvring the point of one's rod one can add a zig-zag action in slow water. I cut reflex devon patterns, with sides painted in contrast to back and tummy ; these show up well and are steady in fast water. The sharp angles prevent the merging of tone which lateral colouring produces in the rounded form. In clear, cold water one can use a smaller devon than usual, if it is spinning very fast. Fast-spinning devons can quickly twist a line, and the two small leads do not exert much anti-kink effect. Therefore we find that it is wise always to have reverse spins at hand.

Nobody can claim that any bait, lighter than the leads which are needed to carry it out, can be cast with the target accuracy achieved by the thread-liner. For trout this is a limitation, but whether the loss is as serious in more open salmon waters, I doubt. I do not think we have many lies on our stretch that cannot be covered from one bank or the other ; none that cannot be explored by the wader. Those of us who prefer the longer rod will maintain that what we may lose in ease of hooking we more than gain in power of playing.

In order to counter this difficulty of casting a bait light enough to fish in the upper surface and yet heavy enough to get out without the need of lead, the late Major T. Ponsonby, so well known to his many friends at Carysville on the Blackwater in County Cork, invented an ingenious solution. He used rag ! Rag well soaked is naturally very much heavier hanging in the air ready for the cast than it is in the water, where it assumes, with its mount, a specific gravity slightly heavier than water, and therefore much the same as that of the wooden devon. I understand that it proved extremely effective in action. I do not know what method Major Ponsonby used in mounting his jumble sale, because on the day I rang up to ask about it I was given the sad news of his death.

The interpretation given here is therefore mine alone. There may be many others better. Here it is : (Fig. 3A).

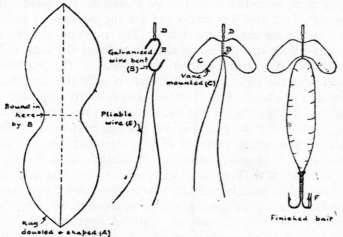

FIG. 3A.—ARMING A DEVON

G

The making of these rag toys is easier and quicker than one might think, especially if enough material is prepared in advance to dress half a dozen or more mounts. Except for swivel and treble the only items needed, besides half a yard of calico, is some galvanized wire (size 19 on an ordinary knitting-needle gauge), some Cellophane sheeting for the vanes, and very pliable wire for mounting. Binding silk and a little fine wire to bind at head and tail, and a needle and thread complete the equipment. Not having to paint means that one can mount and fish a rag bait as quickly as one can tie and fish a fly. I dye my calico, after carefully removing the dressing, with three-pennyworth of some good make of daffodil dye from the chemist. The width is about 40 in., and I tear off $1\frac{1}{4}$-in. wide dyed strips as I need them, making a lovely screech like Smee in Peter Pan. One also needs small scraps of rag for filling or, alternatively, sponge. The rag A (twice the length of the bait) should be twice doubled and then shaped ; a paper pattern is helpful to guide one's initial trials in making the rag skin and in shaping the vanes. The rag will be caught in at its waist by the galvanized wire B. This wire is first bent into a large S to hold the swivel D in a loop at the head. The lower tail of the S is prolonged for the purpose of holding and wrapping round the vane. The rag and the wire E and the vane are placed in the lower loop, the long tail of which is finally turned over the vane. If the galvanized wire is of the right gauge there is no difficulty in forming a neat loop to hold the swivel above, or to grip the wire and rag below. With two pairs of pliers, the vanes, swivel, rag and pliable wire can all be gripped and held in alignment. The waste ends of B are then cut off. If when finished the vanes C seem at all shaky, bind it to the galvanized with very fine wire, and cellire the lot. Sew the rag skin (turning in the outer edge) down one side to the tail, stuff with the rag scraps or sponge, packing them around the wire E, and sew up the opposite side. The treble F is bound in last of all. The closer the bait head fits into the vanes, the better will the spin be. I find that a tapered tail is inclined to spin better, but it might be fun to try something a bit more penwipery in a very strong stream. The method here given is only one of many cadenzas for enterprising virtuosos.

Most people know that Cellophane can be gracefully bent in boiling water and then confirmed by dipping immediately into cold water. I always paint my hook bindings as well as duro fixing them.

A 3-in. rag bait weighs about one-fifth of an ounce dry and doubles its weight when saturated. It is more buoyant than one would expect and would need sinking in the spring. In small sizes, assisted by the merest whiff of lead, one should make quite good shooting and still enjoy just under-surface presentation. I find that the 3-in. type hold better in strong water than do the wooden fellows, but they are nothing like as gay in quieter conditions. I believe they should be quite as good as natural golden sprats, or that expensive alternative of naturals coated in cellire. Their weight should help casting in an adverse wind.

Concerning plugs and wobblers, Miles Furber tells me that the variety of these types that are used in the tropics and in certain states of the U.S.A. far exceeds anything we know of here. Spinning varieties are much less effective there than they are with us. It tempts one to wonder whether this difference is solely due to the difference in the fish sought for or whether the distinction can be based upon water temperature. If fish see better in the warm water, may they not " hear " better, too ? Such easy theories, based upon quite insufficient data can, however, only rank as speculations.

Desperate cautionary tales could be written to warn off those venturing on theories beyond their station. What I dare suggest is based on our register and may only be due to our shortcomings. It is that while rapid rotation, producing considerable vibration, appeals in cold water, however clear and low ; in warm conditions vibration near the bait will repel even in very poor visibility. Slowing down the spin by altering the vaning does no good ; there must be no vibration at all.

Years ago, when I fished for pike, I selected live bait for summer and noisy Colorado spoons for cold and wind. To-day on our water we have documentary proof that in the warm flood-water of summer flies are the best salmon-killers among artificial lures. Only when the water temperature drops seriously do we pick up an odd salmon, or trout, on a devon or other revolving bait.

It would be interesting to know if the same applies elsewhere, and whether the exceptions are few enough to prove that ours is a fairly general rule, or so many as to upturn it.

CHAPTER VIII

BENT RODS

PLAYING a fish is a self-conscious job. Excitement and anxiety undermine aplomb; even if one succeeds in assuming well-bred composure, one hears a thumping heart within. I find it comforting to read of the misery to which Lord Grey admitted at the loss of a fish. Nothing, he declared, can give the same sense of desolation. An ardent young surgeon once turned to me, limp line hanging from his rod : " I feel as I did the first time I lost a patient on the table," adding, " Actually I only thought he'd died ; he hadn't." But this time the broken trace could offer no recovery. Together we sat down and wept.

I remember those pound trout, so much more lively than the commoner grayling, that racked my schoolgirl heart, and are still a loss to me to-day. Playing them my prayers rose audibly, hope and anxiety tore each other to tatters. A pound trout, though it may cause less prolonged tribulation than a salmon, is more electric and inspired. It is not poetic licence which makes those that get off bigger than those which succumb ; the big chaps really are harder to land.

I recall little Peter, aged eight, who used to follow Charles along the river, copying every action, including his worst faults of style. Once Charles found him sitting with the traditional pin and worm and a jar of minnows. Answering the conventional " Anything doing ? " Peter replied, " I larst a big one yesterday." " How big ? " said Charles. " It would have been too big to fry ; it would have had to be biled." He looked up. " And I hadn't even a worm on the pin." Everyone of us has loved and lost something too big to be fried, and with the loss there has also passed away some of our self-respect. Denis is particularly deflating if present at such a mishap. He first tells me, loud and clear, that it was not my fault, and then he begins to brood, unfolding gradually that it was not only my fault from the moment I foolishly chose my hook, did or did not strike, let him upstream, run downstream, brought him in too soon, too late, and too crookedly towards the gaff. More sufferers than I, in unworthy retribution, will remember the day in 1946 when Denis got his gaff home in a fish he was playing himself, only to let the fish pull it out of his hand, injured in an old fishing mishap. The hook had shaken away when the line slackened, and the fish sailed off to the deepest pool, where it freed itself of the gaff, which was never seen again. It had belonged to the General, my father, and Denis was inconsolable. Much as I lamented the gaff—and the fish—the laugh on Denis was almost worth it.

It is difficult to watch or hear of someone else losing a couple of fish running without becoming priggish. In 1946 several friends, a couple of miles below us, had an unusual series of misfortunes, and, of course, the news spread up to us. Fish had torn downstream, on one occasion stripping the reel of a well-known expert and taking away the last inch of line. It was a thread-line, and I fear that I recited the appointed psalm of those justified of erring children. Later other more traditional if less distinguished persons had the same experience of losing fish that tore headlong towards the sea. It was not until the summer, when I walked their water, that the explanation suggested itself. Except when they are too much exhausted to resist the pull, salmon do not often deliberately charge down a fall. Our own stretch is punctuated by many falls, and although a salmon will head upstream into very rough water and court trouble among the boulders, he will generally pause at the brink of a downstream drop. Then, if one immediately walks him back without touching the reel, he will meekly take the hint and be led away from danger. If,

DENNIS IN A LEISURE MOMENT

A "BACK-END" FISH

WATERVILLE, WHERE THE BASS TAKE THE FLY

instead of gentle persuasion, one threatens by side-strain, it will very likely cause him to lose his balance and drift over the edge. This lower stretch, where the downstream series of misadventures occurred, is much less eventful in gradient than we are. A fish, once started downstream, can go ahead ; the faster he speeds the less he tends to be " drowned " by the current. If one tries the dodge of quickly stripping the line off the reel, it will not be carried down quickly enough to create a reverse pull. All one can do is to sprint ungracefully after him as fast as the uncertain footing will allow. Fences, trees, bends, all conspire against one ; it is heavy odds on the fleeting fish. That season, too, the water was low and the current weak. With a stronger downstream flow the fish's breathing would have been affected, and line could have been thrown out after him.

I hope that this apologia may atone to my thread-line friends for anything I may have wrongly suspected of their weapons' shortcomings. To disparage another's chosen gear is more hurtful than belittling his dog ; much more so than decrying his first-born. I have, however, still to be convinced that, except in conditions of bank and bottom which are specially favourable to its use, the very short rod of less than 7 ft. does not lose more fish than will one of 9 to 10 ft. During the first rush it is not possible to cushion the pull by a generous bow of the rod ; one has to let him rip. Indeed, so doing is part of the " tooth-pick " technique. If there is safe elbow room a fish may play itself out, and I can imagine that in a lake or a wide river this free-wheel policy may succeed. There is a world of difference between keeping a whalebone tension with a bent rod and of holding him hard. The pliant rod applies a brake responsive and killing, far more so than a given tension dialled on a reel. With trees, rocks and bank obstacles the advantage of reasonable length is beyond argument. At one time, working a Silex reel, I used a light split cane 8-ft. rod, not for choice, but because, as is so often with me, I happened to have it. Once my fish had finished his capers, I found it very quick for drawing in and still more delightfully easy at the gaff—my weakest spot. Later I treated myself to a spliced 9-ft. 6-in. greenheart, and I became like the fortunate example of before and after using an advertised face-cream. I didn't know myself. Thanks to its nimble flick, I was not only able to cast further, but I handled the first two minutes with more authority. Those who claim, as I used to do, that split cane is intrinsically better for bait have never tried greenheart spliced. There can be no more delightful sensation than the throb of that sympathetic material replying to the demands of a spirited fish. I would not like to swear in court that I now lose fewer, but I would cheerfully assure the jury that, with more length to bend, its feel is less tough. Which comment reminds me of a friend in Africa who was lent a 5-ft. T-L outfit to deal with black bass. " It felt," he said, " like a poker, with an alarum clock on the handle."

During the first frenzy, with line going out, many people stiffen their mechanical reel check. I much prefer a fairly free wheel, checked by hand. Reliance on mechanism deprives one of the personality that comes from touch. Moreover, touch is more sensitive and can be applied progressively. Although the bait rod has more spine yet, I fancy, the longer fly-rod, well bent, has more command. That baits kill quicker than flies is due less to the rod than to the irksome hold and the stronger tackle. A bunch of trebles deep down the fish's mouth keeps it open and is tiring to it. A strong cast and a big spring fly will get out a fish quicker than a small one will later on, with better visibility, gentler water, and fine casts.

Mr. Hutton has kindly given me a table of his own percentages :

	Risen or Touched	Did not take hold	Total	Broken	Lost	Landed	Total
Bait	100·0	13·9	86·1	3·1	14·6	68·4	86·1
Fly	100·0	34·0	66·0	3·2	10·6	52·2	66·0

"These figures show," he writes, "that in the fish landed of all those actually *hooked* there was very little difference between fly and bait. The percentage in each case is just over 79 per cent."

Clearly we know nothing of offers at fly or bait which may occur without a break in the water or of a signal on the hand.

The old adage to keep below your fish is curiously neglected by some modern salmon-fishers. Retribution soon comes if one fails to observe it with trout. The companion counsel of staying *over* him is often bettered by applying side strain. Comparisons in time taken in bringing in a fish mean very little, but some of the favourable results which thread-liners claim may be due to the laggardly ways of many long-rod people. After the first rush is over, they allow their fish to rest and get second wind, or to sulk and get third wind, when a bit of bustling would end the battle. Thread-liners have taught us much in the art of bustling. We all know how unsuspiciously a salmon will respond to being "walked," yet the same principle can be applied without the fisherman moving one yard. A good way to demonstrate this is to play a stick. Throw it well out into a strong stream and reel it in. It will kick and hop and the rod will throb as the stick slowly swings round into the bank below you. If instead of reeling you hold the line against the vertical rod, draw the handle in towards you, and then reel to recover the line, repeating these two actions *de capo*; the stick will skid across the stream to your feet. Thus the old-fashioned cry of "give him the butt" can be usefully applied in a new guise, not in creating an ineffective bend, but by using the handle as a drag. With a shorter rod this technique comes more naturally and largely accounts for the "tooth-pickers'" undoubted success in shortening the final stages of the fight.

There are times when a fish rushes across to the opposite bank, leaving a stream between you and it that tends to belly the line, and if the line be heavy, strain the hold.

By raising the rod well up and lifting the line out of the water and then walking back inshore the fish will be carried back to one's own bank. Since I have toilsomely learnt this knack of moving a fish by drag, I have not only reduced the time in getting him home, but I have thereby steered him clear of rocks and trouble. Side-strain so applied works far more effectively than does side-strain induced by reel alone. The same pumping action exerted skyward—fairly near and over him—will lift a sulky fellow and send him flying off like a dart. When he makes for a dangerous upstream obstacle, it is not safe to try to stop him by holding; picture where his head is and then swing it round, underhand, even when he is on the move, so that he loses balance.

It was during that good season of 1946, when there were fish enough to allow us to keep cool heads, that Charles and I together tried out this drawing-in method. We would watch and criticize each other blatantly, but we would also watch other people in icy and superior silence. No doubt better fishers than we were have always used this pro-cedure, but, judging by the normal lag, I feel that there are enough other mortals left who may not be too proud to try playing a stick. It will at least show that sup-posed repugnance to reel vibration is also shared by inanimate objects.

I gaff for myself so haltingly that I am not entitled to preach, yet a sinner proverbially knows more of sin than does a saint, and so I would suggest that most of our trouble is due to too long a line at the last, and not putting the rod point well behind. If we do this and let the fish drift down we shall not tend to poke and miss so much. Many people, on the Wye and elsewhere, prefer to gaff from underneath with upturned point, but that method needs a wider buttonhooky gape. To me this Cæsarian approach is slightly repellent, and I shall continue to dab at the dorsal fin.

I wish I knew more about coarse fishing, because there

the science is concentrated in not losing. A lost fish means putting down everything within range. With many rivals nearby it is not easy to leave a " swim," probably well ground-baited, for a new one and to start again. If it is competition fishing you may not move at all ; to waste time is disaster. Success depends upon perfect anticipation and touch, which produce the right timing, and on the strength of the strike. The little soft toothless mouth, affords a feeble hold unless the sharp hook is deeply embedded. Many coarse fishers make their own rods, endeavouring to provide just the balance and essential intimacy of touch that will push the pin point well home without risk of a break ; difficult indeed when using cobweb tackle. Game fishers sometimes think that all you have to do when landing a roach, bream or suchlike is to toss it on shore—they don't realize that it plays. Let them try overfamiliarity with a five-pound bream, or still more with a barbel, especially with weeds in the vicinity !

I do not know whether I envy the fisherman who can— and does—recite past adventures in playing individual fish. Perhaps he refreshes his memory with a diary. I remember my horror stories better than I do the others ; therefore when Mr. Marshall Hardy asked me to contribute the tale of "My Most Exciting Catch" to *Angling*, I became paralysed. Actually my most unpleasant capture occurred in the Red Sea on my way back from my first " season " in India. I lay puffing in what one wore in the days before pyjamas ; even that was scattered somewhere under my chin, as the following wind neutralized the effect of the wind-scoop projecting from the porthole. Still, at that age one does fall asleep, however stifling it may be . . . there was a thud on my unprotected body and something cold and wet wallopped across me, from wall to iron cot-bar and back again. I sat up yelping until I heard a bump and more wallops on the floor. I turned on the light and, whimpering with fright, picked up a silver flying fish and hurled it out of the porthole. It was cruel and silly, as the poor creature was bleeding profusely from the wound received when it hit the wind-scoop. Smelling of fish and covered with blood and scales, I lay trembling for the rest of the night. At breakfast the captain was very cross. He relished flying fish—fried.

Moving as this episode was, I did not feel that it would satisfy the hardened epicures of *Angling*. I tried and produced the only account I have ever attempted of how I cast for, hooked and landed a particular fish.

My Most Exciting Catch

Memory, blundering back over the years since my first brace of elvers at the age of eight, has been disappointing. I realize that the best fishing stories are of those who get away and live happily ever afterwards. Frustration, jealousy, betrayal, romantic loss swell with literary possibilities, but success is smug; the captive is now dead—or stuffed.

Had I ever a really exciting catch ? I reflect again, and among the many wraiths peopling the past I can see materializing the relevant and plump pattern of Mr. Wotherspoon—a ridiculous name, but it fitted its owner like an apple skin.

He came to the Slaney as Personal Man to an affluent visitor. Both were as grand as grand could be, especially Mr. Wotherspoon. The guest, escorted by my son, had already speeded to the river in his long Lagonda, while I helped Denis to load a special and appropriate lunch into the ass-cart. Denis Lacey, as butler, gillie and my confederate in all things, was buttressing our prestige in the teeth of ferocious competition.

Mr. Wotherspoon had been showing off snapshots of the pompous mansions he had been visiting, but, under Denis's cross-examination, he admitted that he had never seen a salmon landed.

"HE POKED OUR PETRONELLA PLAYFULLY"

"But I've got my camera for to-day," he said, revealing a large Kodak.

"Only that," said Denis ; "we usually have a coloured cinema."

"Oh! dearie me!" exclaimed Mr. Wotherspoon in a cockney accent that offended our sensitive County Wexford ears. (We believe that we alone speak the Queen's—Elizabeth's—English.) "Only one exposure left! Can I purchase a new roll in your village ?"

"You might try the post office or the saddler," I suggested.

"What a one-'orse 'ole !" said Mr. Wotherspoon. "But," as he poked our Petronella playfully, "I suppose I ought to say a one Neddy 'ole, eh ?"

Leaving Denis silenced, I mounted my bicycle and pedalled to the river.

Air and water were around 48 degrees, but the sun was showing erratically and I greased my line. I had put up a No. 2 Blue Charm by the time the ass-cart joggled up to the river.

"The others have crossed over," I said. "You'd better go upstream and I'll fish below."

Mr. Wotherspoon handed a gaff to Denis. "I should like to see Mr. Lacey give the stroke of death."

I walked off, thanking the Lord that I was alone, and I fished casually down my beat. Nothing happened. I changed to No. 1° Silver Dr. and started to fish the first stream again—deeper. This stand lies on the inner side of a dog-leg ; to cover it one walks along a stone jetty ending in a wooden pier, all running directly downstream. The cast is to the right, with dead water on the left—shoreside—of the jetty. I threw a straightish line and held it in the strong current ; the water was not deep and the fly had a heavy body, lightly winged. It should, I decided, sink enough to be visible to a fish lying low, while the full, fluent teal hackle would give it equilibrium in the broken water. Without moving, I tried a couple more casts at

different angles ; the third time he had it, breaking the
water in the queer way that can happen with a sunk fly.
The fight began conventionally. My spring gear was stout
enough for peace of mind, though the heavy line needed
manœuvering when the fish ran across the stream. I had
worn out a hold before now through letting too long a line
drag in a current. Holding my rod well up, I *chasséd* up
and down the long pier, calculating that, as he was not a
large fish, his first wind must be running low. I no longer
congratulated myself on being alone ; tee-ed up on the
high pier, it is impossible to gaff without an ally. Alongside the top part of the stone jetty the strong water is too
risky. The alarming but best choice is to encourage the
fish to head downstream and then to run in the opposite
direction, reel protesting, banners flying, until one has rounded the jetty on to the mainland to face him again from below.
If, however, he jinks back and puts the pier between you
and him, the line will fail to clear it. This time all went
well ; by the time I was opposite he was evidently slacken-
ing. I drew the butt of the rod inshore and he swung in ;
my hand was preparing to unship the gaff when he spotted
me and shot away into the slack water between land and
pier. A yard or two and he would be under the pier itself.
Applying side-strain, I turned his head and he checked.
Immediately I walked backwards, downstream, and had
drawn him along a precious six feet when—plop—I was
sitting in the river !

I had failed to notice a little bay in the bank, but as the
water was not deep I was chiefly concerned to continue
my successful tactics of walking him backwards. Up I
got ; another and more fatal step. From being waist-high
I was now chin-deep in a pothole, everything submerged
except my head and hat. In my blundering the line had
slackened, whether for the worst or because the fish had
reacted to the suddenly-reduced tension, I could not guess.
Both hands under water, I began to reel in.

"I suppose the i'deah is to coax him into the shore ? "

It was the voice of Mr. Wotherspoon. He was blandly accepting the normal technique of how we play fish in the Slaney.

I continued to reel in and, blessedly, the rod again bent throbbingly.

" He seems coaxed now," I said. " You may as well fetch Denis."

" 'Alf a mo ! "

There was a rattle which I recognized as the shake of a Kodak. For the first time I took my eye off the ball and turned my head.

Mr. Wotherspoon was kneeling. He had the camera in his left hand, the rubber bulb in his right.

" Don't frighten the fish," I stage-whispered. " Put down the camera and fetch Denis."

Responding to conspiracy and the attraction of recording the Matador's final flourish, he lay down the camera as though it were a high explosive and stumbled off as fast as his bunions would permit. I looked at his back ; the camera was facing inland. Still in the water, I reached for and pressed the rubber bulb.

By the time the two men had re-appeared I was standing *nonchalente* in spirit (and body) with the salmon aligned conveniently below me. Mr. Wotherspoon dived for the camera as Denis embedded the gaff and lifted the fish out of the water.

" Steady ! " I saw Denis flinch as the camera was focused upon us, but no smiling film star could have showed more teeth than I did.

" I've got in all the drips ! " said Mr. Wotherspoon, turning the handle ; " *and* Mr. Lacey and the monster."

" Nice little cockfish," said I, suppressing a sneeze.

" It puzzles me, Mrs. Robinson, that you don't prefer to sport waders ? "

" Uncomfortable things," said I ; " they leak."

I handed my rod to Denis. " I'm lunching at the house. Mind you dry the backing."

True ? Well, as regards the fishing part and my immersion, yes. Moreover, we did have Mr. Wotherspoon to stay. For the rest, in spite of everything in the world to-day, fiction is still a bit stranger than truth.

H

CHAPTER IX

"PUTTING THEM DOWN"

DO we believe those optimists who tell us that they don't mind how often other people have fished down a stream before them ? An individual fish, either fresh run or provoked into passion by a recent fresh, is in a suicidal state ; he is apt to succumb to the first temptation reasonably presented. The first time he may, of course, have seen it imperfectly, and therefore be more alert and ready for a second chance. In the heavy water of spring the third time down may be just as good ; indeed, it is impossible to over-fish strong spring water. Moreover, at this season fish are constantly on the move and may come into a stand and rest, just after the first fisherman has left it. Light, atmospheric pressure and the influence of sun can vary with the passing minute ; unpredictable events await us everywhere. Any pool may repay another try with another size and at another angle during those short, exciting days. There is good support for the opinion that, at that time of year, a bait down first may actually excite interest and so enhance the chance of the fly that follows it. Later, when the water clears and warms up, the first fly down has the better, but not the only, bet.

The question whether a bait fished at low and warmer water prejudices the chance of a fly will provoke discussion while there are fish and fishers alive. The ruling on our water, in clear conditions, of fly only before lunch is made by general request. We usually lunch late and rest in the warmth and glare of the afternoon, which postpones late spring or summer bait until the day has begun to wane. Actually our party prefer flies if they are killing, and fortunately they often are.

If there is one recommendation I would make to the

organizer of a party it would be : Don't mix your addicts.
By this I do not mean that individuals should not try both
methods when suitable, but I am sure that a man who always
prefers a bait and will pop it in whenever and wherever
he likes will make the flymen buzz. The plight of a solitary
flyman surrounded by 100-per-cent. baiters would be too
pitiable to contemplate. I never ask anyone to fish our
water without making our attitude clear, and I believe that
the enthusiasm with which this restriction is received
proves that—even as a business proposition—it would pay
elsewhere. It is not a matter of principle, sustained by
known data, but of prejudice ; prejudice holds empires
together when principles have been forgotten. In varying
degrees of certainty fly-fishers feel that a bait disturbs low
water and their nerves fray. Conversely the absolute fly
addict restricts his own scope ; he lacks the variety of
attack which stimulates imagination and should help him
to fish the fly better.

No one who has watched a first-class thread-line man at
work can fail to admire the dainty accuracy of the cast.
" West Country," who never fishes for salmon with a rod
shorter than 7 ft. or with a finer line tension than 6 lb.,
is an example of such precision. It is only very deep-
seated phobia against super-mechanical aids that prevents
me from being a disciple instead of an eye-witness on waters
suitable for playing the fish when hooked.

The unqualified opinion that too hard fishing puts salmon
down is undiscriminating. To admit that the first couple
of rods down are more apt to take the welcoming fish is
not to agree that those surviving are " put down." How
do we know that the majority present were in a sympathetic
mood, have judged and found wanting ? Why, because
they don't like what they have seen, should they necessarily
take an aversion to everything else, especially later in the
evening, when there is so often a general shift of ground ?
Where fish are present and on the take I should always—
if I could—like to roost, only moving off to give adequate

pause and return. When a sulk is on I should go away ; they may come on again presently. Fishing with others one cannot always do this.

The complaint that a beat is being over-fished is usually based on the absence of fish, a factor terribly difficult, if not impossible, to anticipate. The stock may vary, on rivers like ours, from week to week. If there are very few salmon to be shared, four rods are not likely to catch many more than one, unless late in the evening, when a wider assault can be made, and lurking fish may creep into the open. To that extent the water may be over-fished ; but the total catch will not thereby be reduced through fish being put down. Denis is inclined to hold that when the beat immediately below us is heavily prawned that more fish are inclined to run up into our lower reaches. I believe it to be true that bad, clumsy fishing will scare a salmon out of a shallow pool.

It is often held that the presence of many lines passing over them is resented by the fish. Yet all day long flotsam of every description floats by within their view ; sticks, leaves, bits of stalk, weeds ; why they should ever grab at the funny fragments we offer them remains a riddle. Why size of bait or fly should matter sometimes, not at others ? Many lines drifting quietly down a slightly broken stream are unlikely to create a nervous aversion, but it is well within reason to believe that an unnatural action is likely to be noticed and perhaps resented. I had no sooner written this than I recalled the well-known lesson of the summer's day when many fish lay sulking in a pool. After several vain essays a disgruntled angler lay down for a snooze. He awoke to find a couple of lads swimming and splashing in the pool. They dried, dressed and moved off. The fisherman had lost interest in his quest and was only amused when the man opposite unsuspectingly approached with a rod. At the third cast a fish was hooked, and the original fisherman had to sit and watch yet a second one being landed out of the disturbed water.

The presence of swans, of cattle wading, of gaggles of geese may sometimes agitate a stretch, but I doubt that the commotion is more than temporary, and may actually wake them up or move them. I would, however, rather not have a family of swans or a gaggle of geese continually manœuvring up and down my pet quiet stretch. They would certainly upset me.

Which of us has not taken up a strategic position on a bridge and looked down upon the backs swaying beneath us? It is a delightful recreation, but not one on which to base convincing theories on why fish take or why they are scared. Because one fine day we watch a prawn passing repeatedly over a large school of fish without their tearing away, or even batting an eyelid, is not to prove finally that no fish will ever resent a prawn. Those special fish may have been stale, bored or sleepy. They would show the same *blasé* tolerance towards a fly or an old boot, or any object liable to drift down the river. At other times the watcher may see a fish take, or, if the water be very clear, turn round for a scornful look and rejection. The stale or bored fish is not, I fancy, easily scared. The one that is alert and might take is far more prone to be influenced by something he doesn't like, especially if he is lying alone. There is the celebrated stretch at Galway Bridge, where hundreds of fish, many of them quite fresh from the sea, lie in exposed layers. I have not myself watched their being fished, but I am told that it is a mystifying performance; prawns trundle past in procession; sometimes only a head is turned of all the packed array, then, without any apparent reason, there is swoop and—" in him." It would be interesting to note the behaviour of the other fish during the battle; I imagine that unless directly touched they do not break formation. Observation from such a post is fascinating, but it would be misleading to base further conclusions from the behaviour of assembled schools in near tidal water. A fellow that has moved higher up and sat down to rest has become part of the establishment. Local factors affect him and we may now take a vested interest in his possible behaviour, and plan for his assault.

Some quiet situations invite a shrimp, but only when the dish happens to be the *plat du jour*. That in 1946 we should only have killed one out of 144, on a red fellow, and that our neighbours fared no better, trying them even more, shows how baffling the whole business can be. I do not for a moment suggest that the reason we had more fish on our beat that year was because we did not parade prawns so much ; I am nevertheless persuaded that to peg away all day fishing a prawn, without result, is apt to prejudice a possible take on the fly. Fish delight in raising false hopes by mumbling at a prawn without getting hooked ; and so one persists. That their escape occurs so often is a mechanical miracle. On a suicidal day a high average of fish touched are also hooked, even when only a pink fragment is left upon the hook to entice them.

During off-prawn spells neatly sealed brown paper parcels will arrive by post. Reverently they are unpacked by their consignees, the bright bodies straightened, the whiskers combed, before they are buried in the salt or patent dope fancied by their owners. (They look so tempting I long to eat them for tea, but dare not suggest it at 3s. 6d. the dozen.) The consignee still hopes that " they may come on " at any minute. . . . This means that each and every one of the prawns will be lovingly mounted and cast on the waters whilst one whisker survives.

The year 1946 will long be remembered as one of the worst generally experienced—except at a few favoured places, such as the almost unfailing river Moy. It will also be remembered on the Slaney as the dud prawn year. There may be a connection between the cold water temperature and the consequent lie of fish. With no lack of oxygen the heads of streams did not hold as they do normally. Our best strong water stream only yielded one fish. We used to fish the heads blank until we reached where the usual pools are formed ; or we might meet them along the lower ends and deeper water. Undoubtedly prawns and shrimps work best in stronger broken water, although skilled workmen can winkle fish out of quiet places on a shrimp. My resentment for the loyalty people are apt to show in using up their fresh prawns is intensified by the regret that they do not use the worm more or better. Being an object more natural to a fish, it does no harm ; fish that will sniff and turn away will take a fly another day. There are, alas, times when they will not rise to a fly. On such days they have not been " put down " ; they are down already, depressed by a stale, or by atmospheric pressure, or by acid conditions.

Another fear of putting him down happens when a salmon has risen but has not touched our fly. We must give him the best second chance possible ; if that fails we shall still have to try again—but how much more cautiously ! We dare not hammer tactlessly. Most of us mark the exact spot where we are standing, repeating once or twice as nearly as possible the same cast, with the same fly, noting that he may have lain further out and followed us in. How long now are we to rest him ? Should we change flies ? Everyone has his own solution and in rough water it doesn't matter much. One hates to leave a rising fish, but it is not fair to torment him. Some days they tantalize us and splash at us seven or eight times before we win the trick. If we do defeat such a persistent fellow we may surely congratulate ourselves on the discretion of the repeated presentation.

There are some people one dislikes to follow. They lather the water, tearing out the line if they don't like its original angle, and belt it down again. Perhaps the fish really doesn't mind, but one's own morale is wrecked. It at least reveals more neighbourly responsibility to fish out a cast, however poor, than to repair it publicly. Often—though we like to blame the wind for this—the cast hits the water, leaving the fly upstream behind it. To mend at once means a nasty little drag just when a fish may be waiting, but the rest of the swim will be saved, and I think that we should risk the odd chance of offending a single salmon before the line straightens. Mending is one of the attractions of the greased line, no less urgent because we are fishing it fairly straight. It implies inducing the appropriate pace and activity during the entire journey, in a manner that will excite interest, but not provoke alarm. To achieve such a synthesis is to reproduce the flair needed for any form of social success.

Another arguable gambit is the scaring quality of gut. I believe nylon to be less visible and less light reflective than s.w. gut, but whether any particular colour is better than another I don't know. To the æsthetic human eye something tinted looks harmonious. Admittedly pale ones are transparent seen against the sky, and those darkened are opaque, and yet daik ones have helped many people to substantial bags. I always use the thickest gauge my hook will favour, but I try to show the fish as little of it as I can. I don't know how much salmon mind gut. Probably less than we think, unless its shadow obtrudes or its glint is exaggerated. It is much more conspicuous floating, when it bends the surface film of the water into a furrow. I imagine that if one can avoid these bugbears of shadow and glint that thickness does not matter very much. Naturally tiny flies would be inactive if the gut point were gross, but I see no object in using anything finer than the fly will carry, as it is an offence deliberately to risk losing a fish. If gut glint shows up, then rod glint can be followed half a mile away. Fishing into a low upstream sun, I have tried the old dodge of squashing an alder leaf and rubbing on the juice to dull the rod varnish. Fishing a worm in the brightest conditions, Denis never uses nylon finer than 4/5, but I think this would be too coarse with a shrimp.

I always find that trout-fishers are far ahead of regular salmon men in the care they take not to scare. I still have the funny little housemaid's leather knee-pad which my father bought for use on the Avon. Thus guarded, he crawled from ragwort to ragwort, utilizing all the front and back cover he could find. Fellow salmon-fishers thump along one's own bank, or on the opposite side, for choice on the sky-line; they wave their rods to point out where they saw a rise below, disregarding their lengthening shadows looming across the water.

One cannot say absolutely whether any one of such *bétises* has affected our chances, but they reflect a slovenly attitude, and after such a demonstration within my range I always allow a few minutes to pass in order to restore the fish's and my own tranquility. It is one of the advantages of wading that one's presence in the water is absolutely disregarded, even by trout. Danger is only suspected as coming from the bank, and there it is impossible to pay too much respect for ground vibration and to movement on the skyline.

Playing a fish proverbially does little harm, always providing you land him; but to lose one that has been well hooked creates mass hysteria. Rare individual fish have come back again the same day or soon after, bearing the first hook in their mouths, but this does not invalidate the rule that their neighbours have been scared. Trout need resting after a stream has been covered, unless a persistent riser shows again. For some reason they are more shy in some rivers than they are in others, apart from whether they are over-fished or not. I have noticed that where they lie high in the water they are less captious than where they are stationed nearer the bottom.

Again, trout-fishers are scrupulously careful over the colour of their clothes. I imagine that there would be a chilly welcome to a white sweater if it appeared at the Houghton Club. Yet dazzling Alpine effects are common with our salmon-hunters, who claim that they are less visible. In early spring visibility may not signify, although it would always seem injudicious to terrify at the gaff point. Discretion cannot be overdone in more brilliant moments. Choosing one's camouflage offers a delightful excuse for flecked tweeds, gaberdines and becoming hues in stockings. I admit that my habit (fishing solo) of constantly kneeling or of sitting on my newly-captured fish has resulted in a far from glamourous sporting trousseau. If I may anyhow claim that it does not put the fish down, it has that distressing consequence upon my more sensitive relations.

CHAPTER X

LINES AND NYLON

AFTER several years of using nylon as a s.w. gut substitute, fishermen are still much divided in their preferences. Many will never use it at all ; others will never use anything else. There are not many neutrals, although an excellent case can be made for a nylon cast and a s.w. gut point. This compromise also meets the objection that if nylon as a stiffer medium in the water is better for heavy flies, something limper adds life to a small one.

It is not difficult to knot if one masters the simple solutions, five all told. These types counter the two tendencies underlying nylon : (1) that the knot may spring out when tension is relaxed ; (2) that it appears to " cut " where one coil overlies another after tension or a jerk. Comparing nylon gauge by gauge with s.w. gut, we note that nylon becomes progressively weaker in the finer gauges and progressively stronger in the stouter. " West Country," however, has pointed out the anomaly that, for some undisclosed reason, the gauge (014–015) is peculiarly treacherous. We have found it so, at times, near the iron.

It would be rash indeed to discuss this material without reference to the practical experiments carried out by Dr. Stanley Barnes, first published in the *Fly-Fisher's Journal* and now as a most excellent book.* Dr. Barnes, in his many hundreds of trials, went far beyond a straight pull. His knots were subjected to various dynamic strains, and, which is most important with so elastic a material,

* *Anglers' Knots.* Stanley Barnes. Published by Messrs. Cornish Bros.

to prolonged tension. For an analysis of his findings those interested should refer to the originals ; I will only, with his consent, touch upon the ultimate conclusions here.

We have most of us believed that nylon is a more or less constant material, though certainly elastic. Its makers do not consider that it is necessary for us to wet it before we make up our casts. Dr. Barnes has disclosed that the Blood Knot (the only one we should use to join its lengths together) should be tied *wet in hot water*, quickly tightened, and then be allowed not only to cool, but to dry out thoroughly. If nylon be soaked for a quarter of an hour in water at 110° F. it will be more pliable but less strong than normally. If left for a few days it will dry out and recover its strength. A Blood Knot therefore, which has been " bedded " by a quiet strain in nylon soaked in hot water will, after a few days, become so integral with the filament that it will sustain any strain that the filament itself would support. For salmon in the stouter gauges I should still be happy over a Blood tied up on the bank, dry. A bedded knot is less liable to what has been called a " paradoxical " break, i.e. not in the knot itself, but either at or near it. It is interesting to learn that s.w. gut (owing to unequal tolerances in diameter) is far more liable to these paradoxical breaks than is nylon.

Dr. Barnes suggests that the unpredictable breaking inherent in fine nylon, especially in those knots which are usually dependable in s.w. gut) is due to the added internal stresses of so elastic a material. Owing to the elasticity (nylon may stretch to 35 per cent. and s.w. gut to a minor degree) the knots tighten unevenly, and if the coils are very close the nylon will, after sustained tension, suddenly break. He warns us against tightening any knot too violently—finger-pull is quite enough—and against using the " Fisherman's " or the " Barrel." With fine nylon (·013 in. or under) the knot should be made immediately after soaking and then allowed to dry out to obtain maximum strength.

Now for the five knots, plus a variant of my own. For attaching the fly the Turle variant called the Two Circle, the Blood for joining lengths together, the Blood Jam for attaching to swivels, the Blood Bight for loops, and the Blood Dropper, Dr. Barnes has allowed me to use his diagram of the Two Circle, which needs no wetting before

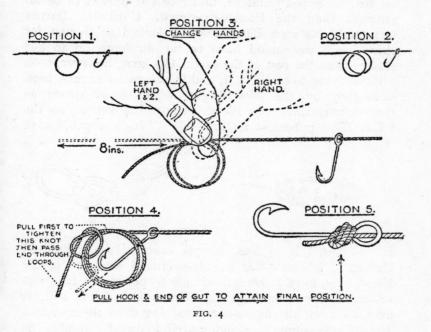

POSITION 1.

POSITION 3.
CHANGE HANDS

POSITION 2.

LEFT
HAND
1 & 2.

RIGHT
HAND.

8 ins.

POSITION 4.

POSITION 5.

PULL FIRST TO
TIGHTEN
THIS KNOT
THEN PASS
END THROUGH
LOOPS.

PULL HOOK & END OF GUT TO ATTAIN FINAL POSITION.

FIG. 4

being tied (Fig. 4). He reminds us that it should only be used if there is room for both circles to fit comfortably round the neck ; but not if one keeps slipping over the eye. With my variant I merely put one turn of the nylon round the fly's head before I tighten the draw loop. It has never let me down.

I rarely go below 6–5 in nylon for salmon, preferring to use a s.w. point, although if the nylon is further from hook or swivel it is safe enough down to 7–5.

The Blood Knot has been described so often that it would be superfluous to illustrate it once more, but the Blood Jam for swivels is shewn (Fig. 5).   There remains the loop, of all the most prone to paradoxical breaks, and much weaker, when the Double-overhand is used, than the Blood.   The neat and elegant so-called Blood Loop was not the answer we had all hoped ; indeed, under test it proved to be no stronger than the Double-overhand.   Until Dr. Barnes introduced his own Blood Loop it looked as though for these knots we should have to tie our loops on to gut stouter than the rest of the cast.   His knot, however, took a lot of tying to make neat, and it has, as he admits, been outclassed by the Blood-Bight, which is as strong as the ordinary three-turn Blood.   I give the version as the I.C.I. have published it (Fig. 6.).   " Its strength," says

FIG. 5   FIG. 6

Dr. Barnes, " is at least 80 per cent. of the unknotted filament," whereas the Double-overhand and the pretty Blood Loop have a strength of only 60 per cent.   It is well to make the nylon loop big enough lest, being stiff, it may open out the figure-of-8 attaching it to the reel line. The tying is simple if enough material is used.   Double the end that is to be looped *twice*, and hold the two ends and the loop so formed in the left hand.   With the right forefinger (placed in the opposite double loop) turn two complete twists ; insert the left-hand loop through the bight formed by the right finger and tighten carefully, so that all slips into place at once.   There is generally some waste end, but time and concentration is spared and, with 40-inch nylon, waste is a luxury that even the most thrifty may enjoy without a blush.

Lady Macbeth could aptly call the dropper " bloody, bold, and resolute." It is more bold and resolute than the waste end of a blood join, and the strain is better aligned. Two turns suffice for s.w. gut, but four are not too much for nylon (Fig. 7).

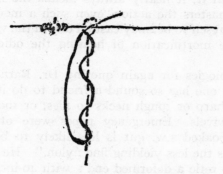

FIG. 7.—BLOOD DROPPER

My own counsel for nylon, and I use nothing else (except a s.w. point), is to fish it heavier than you would s.w. gut. It is amazingly invisible and glintless and its blesséd quality of being fishable without soaking (except for the made-up cast with Bloods) makes it the lazy man's delight. It casts more easily if tapered and in this make-up it is less apt to crack in the casting. A 40-inch length each of 5/5 and 4/5, and a 20-inch top length of 3/5 make a spring cast that will carry all but the heaviest and the lightest flies. Ideally, one is supposed to make the punishment fit the crime by changing for different fly sizes, and so one should —for extremes.

Many people who would like to use nylon find that in casting with it, they crack off flies. I wonder whether this nuisance is commoner with whippy than with stiff rods ? Normally a whippy rod does not crack off flies, therefore the wielder has not to take the same punctilious care to straighten well behind. With a stiffer rod one has to allow an ample lag before making the forward cast, and thus one is more likely to anticipate the trouble and to give the stiffer filament a chance to get round. When I first became possessed of my 13-foot Leonard, which has the spirit of whalebone, I lost about one fly a day for three weeks. When I lend it, it nearly always means the first fly goes. Once one masters the action, even such a moderate caster as I know myself to be, may cast all day in the vilest weather without the mortification of hearing the odious " *pyyk* " behind.

With apologies for again quoting Dr. Barnes (but why think when one has so sound a friend to do it for one ?) : " Beware sharp or rough necks to flies, or too thin ringed ends to swivels. Emergency types were often coarsely finished. Soaked s.w. gut is less likely to be chafed by such than is the less yielding fine nylon." He also reminds us never to retie a deformed end : with 40-inch lengths we may cheerfully cut off and reject the pig-tail.

Since commercial gut sizes are very rarely standard, I give the table of what is most officially accepted :

1/5	- -	·020	7/5	- -	·014
2/5	- -	·019	8/5	- -	·013
3/5	- -	·018	oX	- -	·011
4/5	- -	·017	1X	- -	·010
5/5	- -	·016			

In regard to colour, those who buy their casts ready made-up, to the preferred tint, need not bother, but those who happen to possess a large assortment of lengths in crude white can, at the cost of 1s. and a trifling loss of time, achieve an excellent pale sea-green tone. (" Solacet," fast mist-green, or fast smoke-blue. I.C.I. Industries.) The proportions are given, but the exact amounts are of less importance than timing the immersion.

It is good that an English firm has started to braid nylon casting lines. Recently all had to be imported. Mr. L. R. Hardy has done pioneer work in co-operating

with overseas firms to secure the stuff we want. For bait-
ing, undressed nylon lines seem likely to outclass all others.
In spite of their greater elasticity, they appear to drive
in the hook as well as one could wish, and their endurance
and resistance to friction is remarkable. One rejoices now
to be able to buy them. The one I saw " West Country "
handle so efficiently was white, much the best colour from
the fisher's point of view, and apparently quite popular with
the fish. Most people have their own plan for lessening
the friction where their line rubs the top ring in casting.
I end my line in a long loop, so it is always double at the
critical spot. Denis is most fussy over having a patent clip
attached to the end of his bait line, so that when he comes
home in the dark he has no trouble in unclipping it from
the top swivel of his trace before dismantling. A few line-
drying spools, sited at the point end of the rod rack, save
the bore of unshipping one's bait lines in the evening.
They are too fine to risk leaving in careless coils, with the
fly lines. Miraculously nylon lines need no drying.

It will be even more exciting to see how tapered and
dressed nylon for fly work will compare with the tapered
silk ones. Will they sink in colder water ? The nylon
are definitely much easier to keep greased, as they don't
absorb much water. Greased they will have to be if we
are to observe their meanderings on the surface. The
request, printed in *The Field*, to restore a tacky line has
produced a crop of advisers ; it is not a quick business
and if a professional firm can undertake to get it done, it
is worth the six or seven shillings. To remove the dressing,
dip in the " lime water " used for adding to infant's milk,
or buy some of the cheap pink tablets prepared by Messrs.
Farlow. Once the line is really clean, if you want it to
float treat with cerolene, your own or purchased ; for wet
fly fishing nothing can equal prolonged rubbing with boiled
oil—but it will not be so good for floating, unless applied
by a professional ; and it will take a long time to get the
hard polish we all prefer.

I

Even its worst enemy will admit that nylon has given us a new bone of contention. It has created irreconcilables amongst the closest friends. In acknowledgement of this agreeable diversity of opinion, and in gratitude for all that he has taught us, I dedicate this little story to Dr. Stanley Barnes. It should be appropriate to a doctor if we call it :

POST MORTEM.

The author looked distastefully at the cast handed to him by his kind host, who was collecting gear to replace his guest's fishing kit, which had been abandoned by a female porter at Euston Station.

" I can't endure the stuff," he said.

" Probably you don't know how to use it, Walter," said the ex-Sapper patronisingly.

" Or buy the wrong sort," added the Surgeon. He opened an envelope and took out a long blue filament. " We use nothing else now for our operations. Marvellous tension—resists acid—likes being boiled——"

" Warm as wool," said the Sapper ; " moth-proof."

This tribute was too much even for their host : " Poor old Walter doesn't want a vest ; what he wants is to catch a salmon."

" That'll hold anything ｛he'll hook in your river," said the Surgeon, handing Walter three forty-inch sutures, " only be sure you use a Blood knot."

" I don't suppose the old owl can tie one," remarked their host.

Walter's embarrassment at this just accusation was accentuated by the combined assault of Sapper and Surgeon in their zeal to instruct him. To save prolonged demonstration he pretended to understand, which only meant that he was then shown the Turle Variant, attaching a portly Silver Doctor to the cast, and the Double-Blood

Bight connecting the cast to the line. Purist in all things, Walter was startled by the size of the fly.

" It needed a big eye for you to follow the knot," said the Sapper. " Now you've learnt the method you can easily change it."

Walter wondered. However, he was lent a cob of a rod, a decent reel, and was left alone.

All streams and all fish are alike in print and photograph : we will shun the obvious and not describe the delightful West of Ireland river, but merely follow Walter and listen to him reviling the female porter. Most choosey of mortals, he was now compelled to accept what charity could offer him. The rod got heavier as the day went on, and his spirit even more leaden. The depressing influence of a fly twice as large as the one prescribed in his favourite " Table of Sizes " could not be dissipated by the simple act of changing it. How could he risk his own version of that beastly Turle Variant ? Moreover, Sapper, Surgeon and host all landed fish on smaller flies. With methodical pessimism Walted planted and replanted his Silver Doctor on the ungrateful waters until after sunset, and then . . . Anyone intelligent will fill in the rest of the story. It need only be added that he had never landed a twenty-pounder and that he had always disliked nylon.

At their Sunday supper the mishap was discussed by all *da capo*. No one blamed the nylon. Walter's literary abhorrence of repetition was exasperated by his host's " Poor old Walter." He did not follow the others into the smoking-room, but made the excuse of an incipient toothache to go early to bed. The excuse was genuine, even too true, for presently it compelled him to seek relief in whisky. He went along the passage towards the stairs. The party in the hall below were lighting their candles, but were still discussing his misfortune of the late evening. He halted, unseen in the shadow, in his pyjamas of olive-green silk.

" Was it really as big as he made out ? "

"Quite," said the host; "I saw its back. I was fishing opposite."

"What did he do wrong?" asked the Surgeon. "He was always a bit ham-handed."

"Fingers like sausages," said the Sapper.

"I didn't stare too hard. The old chap was in such a lather," said the host; "he let it get too much downstream."

"His groggy legs couldn't carry his fat tummy," was the Surgeon's verdict. "For years I've been trying to get out those veins. They're like grapes."

"Why won't he let you?"

"Funks it."

"Poor old Walter! Pity no one will marry him." The host led the way upstairs. "I wonder if anyone reads his books?"

Broken morale, no whisky, and a stabbing jaw gave a sleepless night to their victim. He came down to breakfast, his plan defined. The Surgeon, the only one of the party who, in the year 1944, was permitted an "emergency" motor-car, should take him to Foynes; thence he would fly to England to his own dental specialist.

"Drive you fifty miles to Foynes? Nonsense. I'd lose my car licence," said the Surgeon. "I only got down here in order to see a fellow's toe at Innish this morning."

"Our local dentist visits the Innish hotel on Mondays," said the host helpfully.

Walter shivered. *His* tooth: the local jaw-breaker!

"I remember the chap," said the Surgeon; "he was a student of mine. He got his medical, but he took up dentistry. Probably married young."

"I am uninterested in the dentist's love life," said Walter. His tooth gave him a pang, and he decided that perhaps he was. He shrank from the allure of two soft poached eggs yearning towards him on still softer toast. "All right. You may take me in."

Walter's nerves were not placated by the fussy little

"WHAT WAS IT WENT WRONG?"

man, who twittered with his nickel stalked mirror and murmured about a local for his patient.

The patient insisted on a total.

" Heaven help you ! " exclaimed the dentist. " I have not the apparatus for gah-se."

Walter rushed into the hotel bar and pulled in the re-freshed Surgeon, who was carrying his professional bag. The anæsthetic produced from it was indeed total. Walter found himself extended horizontally, mid-air, above the heads of the operators. Dimly he became aware of the Surgeon, washing his hands with the propaganda flourish of one who has finished his job.

" Queer, do you say ? Possibly. Lucky you've got a degree ; but there will be no difficulty about the certificate."

Amidst technical jargon Walter caught the word " vari-cose "—*Varicose ?* The concern of the disembodied patient became acute. He looked more closely below him. He recognized, lying limply on the sofa, his (empty) brown plus-fours. The Surgeon was speaking : " You gave him too big a shot for a single molar. It would have been a waste not to have got at those veins."

" You stitched up a gorgeous seam," said the dentist. " Still and all, sir, what was it really went wrong with the artery ? "

For the first time Walter observed that, lying in the dental chair was a crumpled figure—*sans culottes.*

The Surgeon closed his bag with a snap. " What hap-pened was that the damned nylon gave."

CHAPTER XI

SCRAG ENDS AND BACK ENDS

HOW much in life do we not owe to the unexpected, the unmerited ? We remember the scrag-end of a day, of a visit or a party—the bonus, as it were—not marked on the official schedule. We may have started out looking for one thing and, in unpredictable compensation, struck upon another. It is something to feel that even the back-end of a disappointing life may still reveal unknown but pleasant apparent impossibilities.

Without quick reactions, the best unexpected opening will not itself ensure a Red Letter scrag-end. Among such one can hardly better the miraculous draught of fishes that occurred on the king's highway in Kent in 1944. I have the tale from the beneficiary himself. Mr. J. L. Cooke has called it an answer to prayer : perhaps so, but it also shows how much the enterprising man can help the gods that have helped him. My friend and his brother were weaned on the rod, on the Hampshire Avon and Dorsetshire Stour, until the mess-up of 1914–18 sent J. L. out East. There he fished in anything wet until peace beached him, near the unremunerative Medway. A hard-working married farmer is not going to spare the time or get the cash for fishing far afield. We can picture him on a winter's evening taking down his rod to be varnished, wondering if he will ever bend it again, or stock-take the tackle so carefully stored. For twenty-five years he fished vicariously, through the written word—waiting for the time and chance which may happen to us all. Sometimes he would slink off to a sheltered meadow on a dark evening to keep his hand in, casting at a distant buttercup. Even so, he tells me, enjoyment was cramped by anxiety lest his young daughters would think he had gone crackers.

But time and chance did happen, and to describe it we will refer to his exact words : " The parishes of both Denton and Barham, in which my farm is situated, lie in valleys between chalk hills, valleys that have undoubtedly been, in centuries gone by, the beds of fast-flowing rivers of some size, and I believe there are records to this effect. In comparatively recent years a small stream locally known as the Nailbourne, has on sundry odd occasions run down the Elham valley, through the village of Barham ; the course of this brook, when it does run, being along the roadside that now winds down the valley. On Christmas night the first heavy rain fell, then a very wet winter followed. We had an exceptionally heavy fall of snow in early spring, which was succeeded, before the snow had begun to melt, by a further heavy downpour of several days' duration. As a result of all this the water table began to rise at a terrific rate, springs bursting from almost every hill-side, and within a few days the king's highway once more became a raging mountain torrent, which carved a channel down the valley, including large portions of the road, and flooded several villages *en route*. At the end of March we heard many rumours from our staff, supplemented amply by the grocers' and the butchers' boys, of monstrous trout being seen, all heading up the one-time roadway. At first we were more than sceptical, but finally the rumours became so convincing that my brother and I, no longer able to restrain our curiosity, decided to investigate. We made for a spot where the torrent was pouring over one road, and along another for about two hundred yards. I cannot describe the excitement of two fishermen, who had not handled a rod for years, to see dozens of trout, in fact more than either of us had ever seen at any one time before, all tearing upstream in an endless procession, many of them looking as though they would turn the scales at four pounds and over. It was an opportunity that would

not occur again in a lifetime, so we dashed back for our
rods, etc., which we had not dared take with us, for fear
that the villagers might think we had taken leave of our
senses. Not wishing to start in the village street, we made
for a spot about half a mile above, where a deepish pool
had formed up against the side of the road, before it crosses
this to pour through the hedge on the farther side. Fever-
ishly we sorted out old lines, flies and artificial minnows,
and said a little prayer that ten-year-old casts might hold.
So great was my anxiety to get my line in the water that
I put on the first decent-looking fly that I came across,
but then realized that a cold, wet, windy day was not
exactly fly weather, so I promptly attached a worm on
to the fly !

"Never has my first cast given me a greater thrill ! I
dropped my worm in a gap in the hedge, and let it run
towards the road. At my second cast I was into a beauty
of at least two pounds, and one of the gamest fish I have ever
hooked. My tackle was very old and very light, but, by
what I have always boasted was skilful playing, I finally
got him to the roadside, despite all his efforts to get wound
up in the hedge. Here my brother was waiting with the
net, and I could see that fish upon my breakfast plate.
Alas, the excitement had been too much for us, and no
amount of recrimination has solved the point as to just
whose fault it was, but somehow the line fouled my brother's
boot and away went my trout !

"Thus began two months of the finest bit of fishing we
had ever had. With the farm to run, we rarely got in
more than two hours a day, but were out before milking
in the mornings, and after it in the evenings. Never have
I known so much tackle lost in two months. The whole
course of the stream was a mass of submerged wattles,
tree-roots, and masses of the previous years' dead brambles,
etc., not to mention corners of submerged tarmac which
had managed to stay put at places where the current had
washed the rest of the road away. I lost a large fish with

a considerable length of line on one such place, and also broke the top of my Hardy.

"One thing that puzzled us at the time was the fact that although they appeared to be ravenously hungry, they absolutely refused to rise to the fly. We tried them on everything from gnats to salmon lures, but during the whole time the spate lasted we only struck four, and these all the smallest. The rest were caught on worms or the artificial minnow, both of which they took equally well. Every run and eddy held fish, and I caught our largest on our third day out, a beauty of four pounds, thirteen ounces, in a disused gravel-pit at the side of the road. By the middle of May, when the river was rapidly falling, we had bagged eighty-one large fish, mostly over two pounds. The largest we heard of was 'caught' by the grocer's assistant with a garden rake as it was desperately trying to flounder downstream, or rather road, in three inches of water. It weighed 6 lb. 3 oz.

"The explanation of this windfall did not require much solving. The over-loaded water-table had poured into a fair-sized lake in Bourne Park, several miles below, which was reputed to hold many large trout. I imagine that they had never seen running water before, and had decided that it was a golden opportunity to migrate. Their refusal of the fly was due, I believe, to the fact that the lake was badly overstocked, and practically all the larger ones were thoroughbred cannibals.

"Alas! the 'river that ran again' has long since dried up, and two years ago the lake did likewise. I went over and saw it shortly afterwards; the sight was enough to make any fisherman shed tears of blood. The bottom was almost literally paved with dead trout."

To this account Mr. Cooke's brother had added the comment : "You haven't mentioned, you dirty dog, that you were so mad when I fouled your line that you drove off and left me to walk home."

After hearing this heroic tale we do not resent—we

SOUTH BARHAM
" Every Eddy held a Fish "

KINGSTON, WHERE THEY LOST THE FIRST ONE

CONCRETE PYRAMIDS

actually enjoy—the plunging garden rake that knocked the
six-pounder " on the Old Kent Road." We can share the
staggering incredulity with which the brothers brought out
and fixed their gear and hurriedly added the worm to the
unpopular flied hook. We feel the enthralled excitement
of the first actual tug extracted from " fish out of land."

Even if in less dramatic style than the two brothers,
we may learn from them to be alert, with ear cocked for
local rumour, or for openings, when the fashionable world
has left the waters. At no less exalted a place than the
royal bank of the Dee at Balmoral my parson cousin staying
nearby was granted the doubtful compliment of salmon-
fishing there in August. Those days were well pre-greased
line, and nobody else during that month bothered to try
for a salmon. Yet during those privileged four weeks my
cousin landed thirteen salmon, all on an Alexandra, suitably
chosen, with Edward VII on the throne. He only possessed
one general utility rod—an eleven-foot crooked greenheart,
too long for trout and inconveniently shaky for a salmon.
His funny little reel had no ratchet. The first time I
watched him trouting on Killarney lake he would let his
light line blow away and his flies dance on the water. His
catch was shamingly better than mine, fishing the same
flies from the other end of the boat. The Balmoral assault
must have been one of the forerunners of the floating line.
I never knew such a man for cashing-in on tag-ends. His
argument was simple : " A fish is there—why not catch it ? "

Once, coming over to Killarney, he gave a bad shock to
a stranger travelling with him in the train. Outside Mallow
he went with his black bag into the wash compartment
garbed as a padre ; he reappeared in an amazing knicker-
bocker *en suite*, with a checkerdy tie and a Bill Sykes cap
askew on his brow. As the train drew in he got out of the
compartment with his bag and touched his cap to his
companion, who, black with suspicion, was hurriedly feeling
his pockets. Perhaps it is not astonishing that so many
parsons fish well. They are rarely given an easy wicket,

and have to use their wits for every run they score. It will be a bad day for sportsmanship when lay bank-owners are replaced by syndicates who fail to give a tithe in " days " to enthusiastic local clerics.

For killers, next to clergy and butlers, I would rank schoolboys, their speciality being the unorthodox and freedom from that loathsome word " inhibitions." Late one season a charming lad came to stay with us. I addressed him long and wisely on how and where to fish for trout. He listened respectfully. His father and mother put on long boots, entered the Derry exactly where I suggested and followed my advice to the nylon point. Result, zero. Michael had gone off on his own with a worm. He provided us all with an appetizing breakfast of nice trout picked out of the narrow overgrown head race to the turbine, which had never been fished before.

There can be few rivers which have not dud intervals during part of their season, and it is only by taking a chance at some such time that poor men may happen on the golden half-hours when they may take a salmon. With us our habitual take ends in mid-June, but I have had delightful spells after that date, although I cannot—and nor can Denis—afford time to try in very chancy conditions. Anyone of energy must begrudge heedlessly wasting time that could be expended more profitably. For a person on holiday who likes nature and the sound of running water, it is not idling to linger on an almost forlorn hope. For a housewife, with fruit to bottle and shrubs to prune, it is an offence. To atone for the loss of blank days is the motive behind many of the numerous books written by fishermen ; it accounts for my impertinent intrusion into a form of literature which better housewives have eschewed.

During these wet summer back-ends the rises in the water differ from what one would expect in the spring. Not only does the lusty root system suck in surplus moisture, but the flow is slower over the denser growth. Here we calculate that a March flood, succeeding moderate spring water, will take eight hours to reach us; it is during that spell, especially after dry, cold weather, that we expect to get salmon. The river then falls slowly, nourished as it is by opulent tributaries and brooklets. In June the same amount of rainfall will only create a freshlet, and, owing to the reduced speed of the flow, the rise will often take as many as twenty-four hours to come down. Constantly, after a heavy night's rain, our guests will hurry off to the river, chins high, in hopes of sport. They reach the bank to find the level like that of yesterday and return home disappointed. If they were to adventure down the following morning, the gauge might register five inches up. Unluckily, the few perfect hours of bulging water so often happen at night when we are all in bed. The furtive summer take recalls the climax of a pear, which can only be enjoyed by the intelligent during ten minutes of its life.

The element of acidity, discussed in Chapter XVII, dominates our summer back-ends. Where such exists, there will rarely be a strong grilse run, or take, but luckily odd passers-by often give us a surprise. After June we do much better with a fly than with anything else, including worms. It is useless to bombard stale fish, but if there has been any change that might awaken their interest, there is no nicer form of evening exercise than an hour by the river bank. Next to the obvious stimulation of rising water there ranks a real drop in temperature affecting the supply of oxygen. This is first felt in the air and is more slowly transferred to the water. Then a small fly, fished to show off its blandishments, may suddenly give us the ecstacy of straightening our line. Contact is more uncertain than in the spring. But if he is on, the ecstasy quickly passes and apprehension sets in. One imagines the tableful of sated roisterers at home, making merry of their absent friends. Shall we ever get him to the gaff and thence on to the bicycle carrier? Film producers artfully stage the initial entry of their five figure star. There is no need for such management to enhance his entry when the summer angler makes his simulated *non-chalent* return, carrier in hand. Sensation fills the court. The corpse is identified with some misgiving by those unfamiliar with summer fish. Complexion, contour, above all profile, need tactful explanation, but the proof is in the eating of such a hero (less so with a heroine) and will allay doubts. Boil your water, so much salted that it will float a fresh egg ; drop in the fish while the bubbles are seething and bring back to the same boiling heat again. Then simmer slowly for twenty minutes, or more if the fish is large. This process would even firm up a cod. If you can catch an ugly cock and a comely hen at this time of year, boil the former and give away the latter with your card.

Many rivers have genuine late runs, with comparatively fresh fish, these sweeten the back-end season, although I understand that this run is prone to fluctuate, much as the grilse runs vary.

It is my constant lament that where we are on the Slaney there should be so few sea-trout. If the salmon is wayward, they are more so ; and the few we catch here give us little data, perhaps because we haven't tried at night.

Brown trouters may claim that those who follow the salmon need less skill than they do ; we may retort that anyhow they pursue something that they know is there. We compete against a mystery ; a rising fish does not necessarily mean a taking one, nor a liking for one type of fly only, nor even one which will be there in another ten minutes. After eighteen years on one reach, I learn something unexpected every season. Above all, I have learnt to prefer Query to Theory. The Hunter's inspiration is based on observation of facts guiding to day and to-morrow, and on the experience that anything may happen, anywhere, at any time.

CHAPTER XII

COMBINED OPERATIONS

IT is easy to understand the repugnance felt by many sportsmen at the need for all this co-operation, this planning ahead for the exercise of the most individual of our pleasures. Yet what is the alternative to some form of shared order ? Chaos of the many or unmitigated private ownership by the few ? At present there is a lot of both extremes, but in no department of life can there be a cast-iron solution between freedom and order. Each and all of us would like to own both banks of our own bit of fishing ; enough of it to share with our friends, nice and near the back door, so that we could slip out with a made-up rod when anyone we did not happen to like was seen dropping in for tea. Apart from economic reasons, I should vote for a bit of dry-fly water rather than for a salmon beat. The latter is a Responsibility ; the fish are worth money ; one feels bound to slave all day in all weathers ; more gear is involved . . . and yet ? We must only be thankful for what we have got, or are still able to secure. If in the future we have to share or travel afield it will make for compromise and perhaps benefit our own characters. In Ireland people of moderate means have been spoilt ; there is still so much to be had (for those who know), but even this Elysium will not continue unless we combine to hold what we have and learn to make more of it.

In discussing combined operations we may leave out the Hog. His is a type impossible to suppress altogether, and if we try to fence ourselves in by too elaborate a system of protection, we may find our own style cramped unbearably. Assuming that we are considering joining an association, we shall do better to be sure of the quality of the members before we start adding up the records of the catch. Of what value is a catch if we do not get our fair share in generous company ? Once enrolled, then let us spare no pains to keep out the Greedy and the Boring. Hotel water is more usually a short-term policy ; we shall not get good sport there without paying for it, and very likely we shall not even if we do pay. Once, however, we obtain a reassuring personal recommendation for trout water, we should still take steps to find out about bait-fishers. If we are told that they are always permitted, even in clear water, all possible complication would be avoided, and we need not join. Should we be reassured that bait-fishers are restricted to high and coloured water, then we can lay in some brandlings as well as the flies we fancy. We should also want to know how the water was allotted between guests ; whether it was necessary to race for or to roost upon a stand. Upon the intelligent answer to these questions our booking would depend. If really satisfactory, the price will be high and the waiting list long.

Coarse fishers are well used to such mutual accommodation, and a breach of fair play is quickly resented. Many of the recently-formed reservoirs and artificial lakes in Britain will profit by good management, especially where both coarse and game fish are expected. Hotel managers, working between them a large area of private fishing waters, would help each other and themselves by offering some suitable person his keep and his sport as Special Adviser for the season. There are many retired men of experience and tact who would welcome the scope and interest of such a semi-professional outlet. Off-season improvement work would more than pay for itself, and it would help to employ the best of the boatmen or gillies. Where there are lakes and boats the need for control is paramount. On certain public lakes there is the further complication of visitors owning their own boats, generally with outboard engines ; when these first appeared they, like so many innovations, appeared to be an advantage without any compensating drawback. The weary pulls, the time and muscles saved! To-day are we quite so sure? A lake that could comfortably carry twenty boats, with oars only, would rarely hold drifts for fifteen equipped with the wider range of auxiliaries. The race back against engines more highly powered than one's own means a worse place than ever. Moreover, ignorant or careless people may leave streaks of oil in their wake. The numbers of propellers create a vibration on a calm day, disturbing to the course of a cruising fish that one has marked to anticipate by a deftly-placed dry-fly. If the years of peace and plenty are also to bring a still greater increase in this " amenity," those lakes on which the use is prohibited altogether may gain in popularity.

People who can only manage short-term, day or week-end fishing naturally want to get all they can, and they do not tend to fit in with the longer programme of resident members or guests. Permanent folks know that they will have their turn on the good reach to-morrow, if not to-day. Such short termers are much the most difficult to treat fairly ; zeal may outbid discretion. They should certainly be warned before they arrive of any special local restrictions of any kind. The man who believes that the day's conditions are hopeless for a fly but good for a bait will be impossible to curb if he is suddenly informed of a hard-and-fast ruling against him. It is no use, then, to show him a neatly-framed copy of these rules if he has not previously been told of them beforehand. Equally the fly addict who has to watch a thread-liner catch the rising fish before he has had a chance to cast will be homicidal. Personally, I do not think they should be allowed together indiscriminately. Segregation is far better. It is perhaps easier to cater for the day sportsman on a lake than on a river, provided there are not too many boats and the drifts are allotted.

The quality of the boatmen differ so much that sport may depend upon the luck of having a good man instead of a dud, both receiving the same pay. Duds show reluctance to go out in dirty weather, but none in accepting

K

food and pay for sitting sheltering on an island. Unless
I were assured of the quality of the boatmen who were
to look after me, I would prefer not to go out at all ;
it would only be an expensive and irritating form of being
defrauded.

Regular work for a better class of boatman should be a
sound, economic policy. There are sporting centres on good
lakes which have been ruined by the reputation of the
boatmen. The hotel that is renowned for only recommend-
ing good men would never lack a *clientéle*, and those boatmen
chosen for such a select post would profit by the many
extras they would earn from grateful visitors.

On many salmon rivers where the water inclines to run
low, far fewer rods can be carried at one time than at
another. A balance has to be struck, and it is better not
to overload ; the reverse side being that it must work out
more expensive for the guests. On a river, subject to
changes of level, a good working plan is for the host to
reserve a rod or rods for himself which will only be used
when the water is above a certain datum on the gauge.
This means no waste of opportunity when things are good
and reduced congestion as the scope shrinks. On a fishing
carrying say six rods it is convenient if the beats are
numbered in rotation, but are also bracketted in pairs so
that the two rods can change over after lunch or, alternatively, can fish one behind the other for the length of
the two beats. By sharing, married couples or pals who
divide the services of a gillie can then enjoy elasticity and
cover their bracket between them as they like. If possible
it helps to have a short neutral area as well, near the fishing
hut, so that there will be somewhere any of the six can go
to in bad weather or late in the evening.

Prawning and baits again are a matter for compromise.
Judging by our party, chronic baiters must be less numerous
than one might have imagined. Curiously enough, the
hundred per cent. bait type seem to prefer to raid the fly-
waters rather than to stay together, perhaps because what

would satisfy six mixed fishers would be lean fare for four thread-liners.

Our party gaff for each other and give what mutual help we can. I still feel grateful to Leslie Bishop who got me out of trouble when my rod ferrule stuck. I had no methylated to ease the joint, no match to heat and swell the metal. We even lacked a piece of string. Stuck, indeed! My

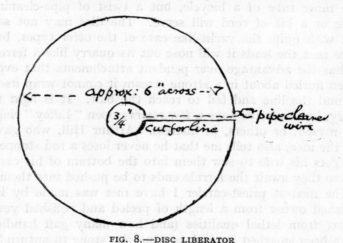

FIG. 8.—DISC LIBERATOR

rod-case was lying on the bank beside me. Leslie picked it up and wrapped one of its tapes round the joint. While I held the rod he worked the tape to and fro, the metal responded to the frictional heat and—hey presto! Such forms of combined operations make the days more pleasant. I have also to thank Leslie for the tip of using Sketofax in cream, or (better) ampoule form (Burroughs & Wellcome's) against midge infliction.

Other useful odds and ends for which I am indebted to my friends include the disc bait releaser, which I now prefer to all rivals. (So, unfortunately, do my guests!) Ideally it is made of light five-ply wood. Give him the material and anyone with the right tools will turn out a couple of dozen for a few shillings. If the five-ply is not to be had, plain deal works, but is clumsier to pocket. The central hole should be of a size to clear the lead, yet jam in the bait vanes. The edges must be smooth and bevelled to spare the line, and the side slit, through which the line is introduced, cleanly sawn. The slit, after the line is inserted, is best closed by a half-inch ring of rubber cut from the inner tube of a bicycle, but a twist of pipe-cleaning wire or a bit of cord will serve. The disc may not sail out with quite the yacht-like ease of the otter types, but once past the leads it will nose out its quarry like a ferret. It has the advantage over pendant attachments that even when hurled about in a strong stream it cannot wrap itself around the line and fail to reach the bait. It is light to carry, but I always have a few reserve open " Liffey " rings for myself, or others, in distress. Arthur Hill, who gave me the idea, also tells me that he never loses a rod stopper. He gets his wife to sew them into the bottom of his case, where they await the ferrule ends to be pushed into them.

The neatest priest-carrier I have met was made by its satisfied owner from a length of peeled and polished yew. Apart from lethal qualities (and how many gaff handles have been smashed for lack of a nearby stone to unturn !), there is no better gag to help in the extraction of a deeply-embedded treble. Even if one's own priest cannot vie with the designed balance of the one described, it is possible to attach some line which will endow it with the dual purpose character of executioner and undertaker (see Fig. 9).

On some rivers where kelts run late, gaffing is prohibited in March. I regard such a provision as monstrous. Goodness knows salmon-fishing is hard enough to find, and dear enough to secure, without imposing an extra restriction which would compel the employment of a gillie.

The problem of gillies and of their tips is one that will need much readjustment in the lean days ahead. No one wants to be stingy, but to " spoil the market " for others is even more selfish. A guest staying free and gratis is

often terrified of letting down his host by not giving satis-
faction to the privileged staff. His visit may easily cost
him more than if he were staying at a fixed rate and selling
his catch. In pre-1914 days an acquaintance of mine was
invited to stay with a rich friend on a renowned Scottish
river for one fortnight. Before starting he took the pre-
caution of consulting the firm from whom he bought the

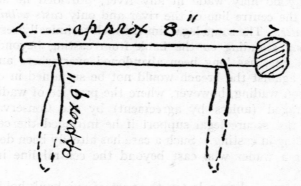

PRIEST CARRIER

special gear needed. What were the tips expected by the
head gillie and the two boatmen necessary for each rod?
The answer was unequivocal: for such a period, twenty
pounds to the head gillie, and ten pounds to the boatmen.
This was apart from house tips. It is to the credit of the
gillie and the men that when my friend explained that he
was a hard-up soldier, they served him cheerfully for half
this figure. If anglers knew that such services were not
part-time seasonal jobs, they would not feel bound to tip
at a rate that would soon make fishing prohibitive. The
habit of giving drinks after a fish has been landed is also
demoralising and helps to create a parasitic attitude, and
a loss of dignity. People, too, who prefer to fend for themselves, should not be embarrassed and eyed askance by the

local staff. If sport is to be more fairly shared and less an affair of personal privilege, the tipping business should be levelled out.

Wading is another topic for controversy. Some rivers cannot be fished without wading and there is reason behind the claim that wading disturbs the water very little. On the Slaney it is not allowed unless both banks are under single control or both holders agree to the practice. In law anyone may wade in any river, provided he stands inside the centre line of the river and only *casts within his own water*. The same legal limit, which technically restricts a person standing *on* the bank from casting beyond the central line, has long been abandoned everywhere and an action against the breach would not be sustained in court. A person wading, however, where the practice of wading is discouraged (unless by agreement) by the Conservators, would not secure legal support if he infringed the central line ruling in casting. Such a case has already been decided against a wader who cast beyond the central line in the Slaney.

This non-wading rule (on the part of one bank holder) is upheld very rigidly with us, and I for one would resist a change. Except at a very few places (nowhere on our fairly narrow beat) one can cover most of the streams from either bank ; the few that are better fished from one particular side give welcome privacy for that party. To have a strange *vis-à-vis* walking down the middle of the river and picking out fish from under my toes would cause me great annoyance. Many elderly people dislike wading· and would be put to a disadvantage if those opposite them were to do so. On our beat we do all we can to provide suitable jetties for the dry-footed. When we happen to hold both banks, our party fit in with each other's idiosyncracies, and wade or not by consent. At very low water, wading gives enormous advantage to the fly. One can hang a short cast downstream and not disturb the lie by showing the line. But, even admitting the loss of this strategic approach,

I would not submit to any casual *vis-à-vis* disturbing a convention which has existed for so long on our river.

In most dry-fly trout rivers such a convention would not be disputed, even when both banks were under single control Woe betide any stranger who defied the tradition of the residents ! Local rules are generally founded on some reason and maintained by consent. The prohibition (on a few rivers) of very fine gut points for trout may mean that without it too many fish are lost ; or that to be successful 2X demands a higher standard of casting than does 4X. Even on some salmon waters only artificial baits are permitted, which rules out prawns or worm. If aspirants to join don't like it, they must go elsewhere. Casting into the brown, instead of for a rising trout, is bad form on rivers where a good rise may normally be expected. To observe so chaste a restriction on the trout streams around us here would be comical ; although I sympathize with the K.C., who is opposed to indiscriminate downstream trout fishing with a wet fly. He says that such a slap-dash method means catching small fish and pricking others. But since the upstream art is harder work, I rather fear he will not have as many followers as he deserves. Returning small brown trout, where such abound and there is no defined limit, depends upon our subtle sense of fair play. I have no reluctance to keeping eight-inchers. Anything less looks humiliating when fried. On those days when trout are conspiring to kill themselves it is only massacre to keep more than a good feed for the party.

Fishing contretemps are no more frequent or ill-humoured than those in other human relationships. Still the Bishop (who told me the story) agreed that he envied the unilateral action of the cross man, who for years fought with his fishing *vis-à-vis*, Mr. Clancy. " Haven't they buried the hatchet ? " asked someone. " No. They buried Clancy."

In most things David Harum's maxim, of doing it to the other fellow " fust," is hard to resist, especially if (like David) one is perfectly sure that the other fellow would do it unto you, if he could. It is trying to be asked to reveal the precise copy of what—after much seeking and ingenuity —one believes to be the only poison of the day. It is agonizing to leave the fish one has just risen, so that the Enemy may have a chance at it. It is frightful to have one's eye well and truly wiped in the presence of many witnesses. Those who pretend they don't mind such things are either liars or insensitive. To mind, but to struggle to get on top of it is the best to which most of us can aspire, while still fishing in territorial waters. Beyond the strato-sphere we may be in a better state to follow the ruling given by St. Peter, the Netter :

" Love the brotherhood : be pitiful : be courteous."

The next chapter will illustrate one of the curious com-plications that may arise even within a most friendly and co-operative party.

CHAPTER XIII

A FISH FOR SOLOMON

THE Colonel rang-off the telephone and joined his wife in the drawing-room. "It's the Thompsons," he said. "They want to come down this evening and fit in a day's fishing on Sunday before the first. The first is Monday."

"There's nothing for them to eat."

"They're bringing a ham—cooked."

"Oh, well, I suppose that's all right. When do they get here?"

He looked at his watch. "At about nine. They were starting from Dublin at once."

"Just time for you to catch me a fish before they come. We needn't say anything about it to them. Mother'd love one."

"Pretty hopeless. Old Morley hadn't had a pull for the last week. That's why he left before his time was up."

"He only uses a fly and that's hopeless this weather."

"There wasn't a prawn in Dublin, but I'll do my best with a worm."

"Do. You know how much mother likes a salmon. I'll have a dish in readiness for the Tommies, wreathed in lettuce and beetroot, with a hole in the middle for the ham."

The Colonel hurried to the river, but his worm turned in vain. It was annoying not having had time to order prawns, but his tenant had left too hurriedly. However, why grumble at getting a few bonus days at home with no loss of rent? Normally Mr. Morley's tenancy would have ended on the last day of April, which happened to fall on Sunday, to-morrow. His friends, the Thompsons were booked for May. He had readily agreed that, as the next tenants, they should anticipate their stay by arriving that evening, plus ham.

Letting their house was a convenience to the Colonel and Madge, since they could always go to her mother living the other side of the county. Letting the fishing was a sorrier wrench for the Colonel, but on it depended letting their house and staff for a lucrative three months. Only what the Colonel called " circumstances " (actually keeping their boy at an unnecessarily expensive school) induced him to make the sacrifice.

The Thompsons arrived in their old car filled with rod-cases, and a trailer piled with the distorted shapes of household and personal luggage. Thompson disassociated himself from everything but the rods. His wife, he explained, had invited an infernal party on Monday. He was longing for two days' quiet to shake down first. The Colonel and Madge must promise to come to them for another week-end, to make up for this one.

" Where's the ham ? " said Madge as she led the way into the house.

The following morning the Colonel conducted Tommy to the river to introduce him to the stands. He himself did not take a rod, preferring to be free to point out the various peculiarities.

" Just for to-day," he explained, " we have both sides, because Morley also rented the opposite bank from the Admiral. From to-morrow, with only one bank, you mustn't wade, and you mustn't bait before tea. The Admiral's a nice old boy, but quarter-deck over agreed conventions."

Tommy assured him that he never waded and much preferred flies, although at the present state of the water, he, too, lamented the dearth of any prawns in Dublin.

" They had nothing smaller," he deplored, " than bottled lobsters."

They walked to the head of the beat, but before it was reached they came upon a tall, gaunt man playing a salmon.

" Good work," said the Colonel. " Would you like me to gaff him ? " With the fisherman's approval the Colonel neatly slipped in the gaff and knocked a nice 10-pounder on the head. The tall, rather solemn man thanked him and explained that he had been early on the water as he was going away for some days. He hitched his carrier to the fish's mouth and tail.

" I see it was on a prawn," said the Colonel. " If you're going away, I suppose you couldn't leave us some ? "

" Unfortunately, it's my last. If I'd lost that I shouldn't have got this fish, which I need badly for the friend I'm staying with. I'm so sorry."

" *Slán agat agus go neirige an t-ād leat a cara an t-slat iasaig.*"

He walked off.

" What's he saying ? " asked Tommy.

" Something polite in Irish,"* said the Colonel. " He's one of those professional Gaels, but quite a decent chap if you know how to handle him. It's a bit touch-and-go between him and the Admiral—the Admiral's water runs opposite to him for a couple of pools above us. The Admiral kept that bit for himself, and didn't let the part above our bounds to Morley."

" You might explain our exact boundary. I thought the Gael fellow was actually on our water ? "

" He was when I gaffed his fish. The stream is divided by that broken-down bounds fence. We have an agreement that we cross the fence at will to play a fish, as they are inclined to run up and down the stream."

" I'm glad you came with me," said Tommy ; " it's puzzling."

He put on a fly and fished slowly down from the bounds fence, the Colonel expatiating on every stone and eddy on the stretch.

Madge and Mrs. Tommy were waiting in the hut with the lunch.

---

* " Good-bye and good luck. Friend of the fishing rod ! "

" Who do you think has turned up ? " said the latter to her husband. " William. He's fishing the pool below us. You should just see him."

" Who the devil's William ? " said the Colonel, who was beginning to wonder if there was going to be any river left for his last day.

" One of the Brewers," said Tommy. " Nice, but a bit big for his boots. They get like that. I'd told him we were coming down and to look us up, but I never expected him to come to-day."

" He is going to Galway to-morrow. He rang us up at home and found we'd left, so he thought he'd look in here on his way. He leaves very early to-morrow."

Tommy thanked the Lord out loud and the Colonel in silence. They had hardly sat down to lunch when William walked in. He was fair, with a good-humoured, shiny red face, and he was wearing what looked like a complete diver's outfit in bright green.

" My dear lad, what do you think you're doing in that ? " said Tommy after he had introduced him.

" It's new. Hardy's very latest, made of plastics. It weighs about half a pound, has spliced gussets, and secret pockets, and——"

" Sit down and eat something to fill it," said Mrs. Tommy. " I don't believe you're even allowed to wade here."

" Not after to-day," said the Colonel, as he recited the conditions over again.

" That won't worry me," said William, " as long as I can christen this with total immersion to-day. I've got a marvellous new prawn mount."

" Have you got any prawns ? " duetted the Colonel and Tommy.

" I'll leave you some to-morrow, if I've any left over."

The Colonel and Tommy accepted this semi-noble offer in semi-noble gratitude. Before they had finished their cheese William got up and declared his desire to be on the water again. His special prawn mount was designed for

"GAD! HE'S CARRYING A FISH"

the brightest sunshine.   Rather curtly, he was told to find
his way upstream ; since the Colonel wished to complete
his conducted tour of the lower half.

They waited for the glare to leave the water and were
about to start when William, looking like a large wet frog,
was seen galumphing down towards them.

" Gad ! He's carrying a fish," said Tommy without
enthusiasm ; " the twin of the one we saw landed this
morning."

" Where are my prawns ? " shouted William from afar.
" I must have left them in the hut ! "   He shuffled
past the party, handing the fish without comment to the
Colonel.

" They're not in here.   You must have eaten them,"
said Mrs. Tommy.

" Of course they must be there.   I haven't got them.
That salmon simply munched it up on sight.   They won't
touch anything else."

A fruitless hunt led to the only reasonable conclusion
that, in the excitement of playing the fish while wading,
the prawns had been washed away.   A deflated frog returned upstream, holding a tin of distasteful worms, while
the elder men continued down below.   There was no other
incident, although they all fished till dark.

William, in his long gleaming open car, left early on the
Monday morning.

The obsequies of departure ran their accustomed course
and the Colonel and Madge agreed to return for the week
end of the following fortnight.

" You mustn't forget to take the salmon," said Mrs.
Tommy.   Mutual politeness resolved on the obvious compromise of half and half each, to satisfy Madge's mother
and Mrs. Tommy's party.

" I'll get Mary to cut it," said the Colonel.   He rejoined
them shortly.   " Mary says that the gentleman took it
away in his car."

" How like William ! " said Mrs. Tommy.

" Well, perhaps as he'd caught it he thought it was his," said the Colonel, picking up his post which had just arrived.

" Inexcusable," said Mrs. Tommy, " slipping off like that without asking a soul."

" It was early to wake anyone up," said Madge.

" Nonsense," said Mrs. Tommy. " There should have been no need to ask. Our rights don't start till the first. The fish was yours."

" Nonsense," said Madge. " We took your tenancy as starting when you arrived. The fish was really yours."

" Anyhow, it wasn't William's," said Mrs. Tommy. " I suppose he hopes to make himself popular with his rich friends in Galway."

The Colonel interrupted : " You needn't worry over the fish any more. Here's a letter from Mr. Morley, asking me to post him a salmon if we got one on or before the thirtieth, of the right weight. William's fish would have filled the bill exactly, so neither of us could have kept it."

" I suppose it legally is Morley's fish ? " said Tommy.

" Clearly, since he was still paying the rent," said the Colonel. " Luckily he won't know about it. However, anything caught from to-day is yours."

A fortnight later the Colonel and Madge returned for their week-end. The weather had remained " perfect " and only a couple of fish had been taken (on prawns).

" Any news of William ? " asked the Colonel as the party collected for evening coffee.

" Not a word," said Tommy.

" He's getting just like Toad of Toad Hall ! " exclaimed Mrs. Tommy. " In those ridiculous green crawlers and that long shiny car."

" I'm afraid," said the Colonel, " that the fellow's been getting me into hot water "—he took some letters from his pocket—" here you are, *Exhibit A*. Letter to me from the Gael, beginning *A Chara*. He points out (in English) that the British Admiral had been extremely offensive and abusive because, on April 30th, a so-called sportsman had deliberately entered the river from his (the Gael's) bank and had then waded and hooked and landed a salmon. The Gael goes on and on, ending, ' you will agree that on the circumstances I am entitled to the salmon—or its value. *Mise le meas.*' "

" Damn William," said Tommy.

" Amen," said the Colonel, " but I blame myself for not showing him the exact bounds. That's not all. Listen. *Exhibit B.* Copy of letter from the Admiral to my late tenant, Mr. Morley. The Admiral writes in hissing rage because he has been made look a damn fool before that Irish bloke. All due to one of Morley's party, who, on April 30th, had been poaching from the Irishman's bank. Not only that, he had been wading on the Admiral's side and had killed a fish before tea on a prawn. The least that Mr. Morley could now do was to hand the fish (or its monetary equivalent) to the Admiral Finally, we have *Exhibit C.* Letter from Mr. Morley to me suggesting that I might like to send him thirty shillings, adding that he could not but feel it was somewhat discourteous (as he was still paying me for the fishing and the house and staff) that I had not voluntarily posted him the salmon as requested."

" To think of William and his rich friends sitting guzzling it ! " said Mrs. Tommy.

" What's that ? " said a voice behind them. It was William returning on his way back from Galway.

" But Lord bless us, I've never seen the blasted fish since I gave it to the Colonel ! " said William.

Omnes : " Then where is it ? "

William turned to the Colonel. " I gave you a lift back that night in my car, sir. I heard you put some stuff in the boot."

The Colonel gave an uncomfortable gurgle.

" But surely, William," said Mrs. Tommy, " you must have unpacked it that evening at the house ? "

" It was dark. I just took out my waders to be dried. The maid pushed them in again in the morning."

" But you must have emptied the boot in Galway ? "

" Why ?   It was far too hot to fish."

The Colonel picked up a torch and they all followed him on to the sweep outside the front door. In the pencil gleam of the torch William's silver car looked spectral. The boot was unlocked and opened.

There was no need of light to assure them that the salmon was still inside.

The torch conveniently showed up the green waders, which William snatched passionately from the affected area. He held them out at arm's length by their toes and a shower of pink prawns tumbled from the secret pocket to mingle with the general aroma.

L

CHAPTER XIV

" THE PLUS SIGN "

(1) *Stock Betterment*

LOOKING at what, admitted misapplied, science has taken, we may well ask has she anything to give us back in exchange ? We are told that in the United States there is hardly a fishing river running into the Atlantic that is naturally stocked. The many fishers there are duly provided with reared fish, nourished by hand and replenished from year to year. In the future Englishmen may be thankful if there are even clean rivers left to replenish. Undoubtedly, by the development of hatcheries, fry should be procurable ; how far can the qualities of rivers or lakes that are to hold them be improved ? Biology, based on chemistry, geology and nutrition, is now grouped, for purposes of fresh-water life, under the single term *limnology*. It is to the experts so engaged that we (in both islands) shall have to turn for future enlightenment. All this may sound remote and quelling, but we may comfort ourselves that for reliable data scientists still depend on responsible fieldwork undertaken by sportsmen. The greatest authorities on pisciculture in England to-day are undiplomaed scientists like Mr. Arthur Hutton, Mr. Calderwood and Mr. Menzies, certainly in knowledge of game fish.

The latter two authorities are associated with the experiments being carried out in Loch Sween in Scotland, where plankton mosses on which the fish feed are fertilized. Results here, as in North America, are promising, and should increase the market supply of fish. Rods are more likely to benefit by the newer views on acidity correction. Crushed limestone (not burnt), which may be obtained from road-breakers, is placed on to the river's floor. It has been whispered that some such expedient has been tried out at Inver in Connemara, with dramatic improvement to the weight of the sea-trout. Such advances would be real and welcome even if their application was limited.

Whether private ownership is to continue or not is to impinge on politics, but while it exists its value to fishermen will be judged by the results it achieves in improving the potential under its control. Closer co-operation for stocking and weed clearance is an urgent need. Experience is unanimous that a natural balance must be maintained and that it is dangerous to try to better the good. We shall do well if we even succeed in keeping it good. Experiments in introducing new-comers from overseas are rarely worth while. There are enough of our own at home. If half the enterprise in launching rainbows had been spent in looking after our existing streams, there would have been less disappointment. The few successes in England are cancelled out by the list of expensive failures. One reads heated correspondence over the advantages or dangers of swans, herons, otters, etc., etc. The answer is rarely Yea or Nay. (Except, I should hold, against that obscenity, the Cormorant.) That balance of power which Wolsey recommended for Europe may be out of fashion to-day, but the spirit of its lesson persists. Perhaps it is the word power which has properly become suspect, nevertheless, in every human activity there has never been a time when the quality of balance had been more important. Replacement of tooth and claw in jungle life is now sought in alternatives based on statistical propriety, but if the ultimate product be not properly poised, unforeseen consequences may shatter the most amiable intentions. Local fauna and flora must make the best working laboratory for small-scale experiments, based on water and food analysis. A short-term policy may prove a long-term blunder.

The old saying about gaining on the swings what you may lose on the roundabouts contains the concealed warning that it is well to know which of the two you want most. It would, for instance, be foolish to sacrifice a good supply of coarse fish in an attempt to improve the trout stock, unless one were sure that the character of the water was likely to suit trout. Any experienced person, knowing the geology, the depths and observing the weed formations would have a shrewd idea. On the Severn, where the coarse fishing is as valuable, if not more so, than the salmon-fishing, very careful adjustments have to be made. On Windermere the Freshwater Biological Association have carried out most interesting experimental work in netting (for canning) the abundant small perch population. Already the effect on the growth and number of that rare and elusive *salmo* variety, the char, can be followed. Now the balance has once more begun to hover ; only experience will guide future steps and maintain the perch and other stock in right proportion.

Pike give such excellent sport that, in certain deep stretches, it would not be a social act to destroy too many. It is where trout and smolts run that pike can become a menace, as they are no sticklers for the deep regions if off-points rations are to be had in the shallows. The presence of abundant perchlings a bit too early may distract big trout from their proper annual gorge on green drake. One year's weather may favour one development and spoil the next ; only a man of wide and long local experience could hope to gauge the portents.

Propagation by hatcheries is unlikely to improve much more except in detail. The increasing reliance on natural process grows. Aristotle's rivershed eggs are coming back into fashion. He used to collect masses of weed banks containing fertilized eggs for his hatchery tanks. The belief that artificially-hatched eggs meant less loss than occurred on the natural unprotected salmon redds has recently been shattered. Instead of prodigality, nature here shows extreme thrift in material. Nearly all the natural eggs are fertilized ; they are not washed away by floods (except in rivers like the Spey, where the course entirely changes beds), and they are unbreakable. So deeply are they embedded by their parents that when Indian ink was released in the stream above the redd, none was seen to penetrate through it. Their enemies are their own kind which spawn late and kick up the carefully-engineered beds, and trout which gorge on any that may be misplaced. The alevin and fry ages are known to be the dangerous ones.

Dr. Knut Dahl of Norway introduced the theory that big eggs produced quicker growing trout. (Gardeners also would choose well-developed seeds.) Latterly rearers incline to favour the belief that after the first two years of life environment is the controlling factor, though the large eggs and a prosperous first year will hasten growth. Where it can be given, natural food is not only better for trout than stew feeding, but it may promote better risers to fly. Mr. F. E. Sawyer with fly-boards and Mr. C. Myers with Plankton have been supplying their charges with midge larvæ, and find it simpler, cheaper and better. Liver appears to be the most recommended alternative. I have kept little brook trout happy for short periods on grated carrots and a sod of grass turf. It is most important that rotted food should be taken away by the current and not left to decay. We also need to know more about the influence of phosphorus and iodine on promoting growth.

Mr. Norman Weatherall has given a diverting account of what he calls " Trout Gastronomics."* A six-ounce trout was found to contain twenty-six good-sized minnows and four black slugs. Another had eaten fifty earthworms, while a 14-oz. trout contained a toad, two bullheads, two young water rats, six caddis cases, and one larva. They appear to dote on mice, and have taken vipers, crayfish, bats, chaffinches, potato peelings, a young duckling and a tabby kitten. What a shock to those of us who believed them to be fastidious !

There can be little doubt that our breeders will be able

* *Angling*, Oct., 1946.

to supply the demand for fry of appropriate size to release if suitable waters are there to welcome them. Food improvement in streams and lakes again is an affair where advice can be found if it is sought. Lack of this knowledge led to the overstocking tragedy told so movingly by Mr. Plunkett Green in his enchanting book, *Where the Bright Waters Meet*. Alkaline water is known to produce the fatter trout, but also more natural enemies. Where new reservoirs are formed a little care in their construction may make the difference to their fishing stock. Steep concrete sides provide no agreeable margins for vegetation and insect life. Where it is possible variety in depth is welcome ; in summer a large shallow expanse loses oxygen, whereas deep water alone means poor risers and few weeds. For trout there must be present running streams feeding the lake to allow spawning to be carried out. It is here that vigorous protection will be needed against every type of predator.

My friend Captain Digby, who keeps a hatchery as a hobby at Milltown, near Dublin, tells me that among birds the kingfisher is the cheekiest and most dangerous to the breeder. It is not only small enough to slip through a crevice, but it has abnormally keen eyesight and will fall upon the most obscure victim. The heron lacks this acute sense of vision, but will hover when it sees a kingfisher at work. Once the smaller bird makes its pounce, the heron knows that the going there is good and pounces too.

My other hatchery friend of long ago, Mr. Arthur Severn of Bibury, had the same fear of the kingfisher. He must have been one of the earliest breeders to prefer the natural to the synthetic. He would warn me of how carefully one should handle the smallest fish before restoring it to the water. He ascribed the darkness of many fish not to blindness, but to mishandling when young. A pinch behind the gills, he said, would affect the pigmentary glands and injure subsequent growth. Trout are rarely " returned " in Irish rivers—and black ones rarely seen !

After recording this memory, I came upon some comments of Mr. F. E. Sawyer on black trout, written over thirty years after Mr. Severn had made the observation to me. He writes : " My investigations have suggested to me that blows on or near the lateral line, in a certain part of the nerve system, destroy the pigmentation system of the trout and also affects its sight and then the colour. But while the majority of black trout are blind, no positive rule can be laid down, because some black trout are not blind ; also the majority of blind trout in a river are not black."

The blows to which Mr. Sawyer refers are more often those dealt by a heron's beak. Injudicious pinching may, however, be equally harmful to a small fish.*

Filling up old gravel pits with water would seem to provide a chance to make something out of nothing where the inlet supply can be maintained. These are more likely to succeed for coarse fish than for trout, as they are usually too deep for weed growth and lack inlets for spawning. Where circumstances should favour trout, it is a mistake at the same time to stock with coarse fish. If this is to be done, let some of the trout mature first.

For the game fish, however, the problem is less that of discovering the new than of preserving what still exists. Above all, the dredger needs a jealous eye.

If the betterment of fresh-water non-migratory stock is not the mathematical business it might at first appear, what of those species that are only born at home, then spend their maturity in the unknown ocean, returning for their nuptial climax ? What of the reverse eel emigration ? How far do these aliens, born and mated abroad, affect the balance of other fishes during their eight or ten years' gluttonous sojourn in our waters ? Because they provide so little amenity sport, we might like to ignore them, but we cannot ; their food value makes them an important commodity, and their existence is a natural factor in the

* " Black Trout, Observation on Injury by Herons," F. E. Sawyer, *Salmon and Trout Magazine*, January, 1947.

balance of our rivers and lakes. We do know enough to assert that the practice of long-line fishing (even if reduced from 1,000 to 350 hooks) should everywhere be replaced by the ordered methods of weir traps. Future direction by lights may make even these modern devices obsolete. Long lines can only capture immature, yellow feeding eels, which will not keep and which lack the rich condition of the silver adult, ripe for its ocean fast. Long lines have the additional objection that they attract big trout. A universal restriction would not only improve the marketable product, but its practice could be regulated to conform with other fishery policies. Granted compensation to line licensees, the advantages gained by the power to control the silver eel output is one of the few certainties in betterment.

How far salmon hatcheries are worthwhile is disputable. We know so little. How much does like breed like ? Can early runners be effectively introduced into late rivers ? Because sometimes this appears to have been effected is not proof that it will always work. How do we know that the selected hens are early runners, or that the milt came from an early cockfish ? It would, however, seem that each river is inclined to produce the runner that suits it best ; this is the opinion of Dr. Knut Dahl. Anyhow, admitting that big rivers have bigger fish, why should their smolts know that they can safely enjoy a long absence in the sea ? I am always uncertain of anyone who claims definite success from introduction of " outside " stock to alter the character of the run. The Conservators of the Ribble have made out as good a case as any, and yet since indigenous fish were present, can we be certain that the better protection which these received did not contribute as much as the new-comers to that river's recent recovery ?

An entertaining story is told in Canada of how the authorities controlling the hatchery on a renowned Canadian salmon river sold a large consignment of marked fry to the board of a neighbouring river in the States, where stock was deficient. The fish arrived and were launched in the American river. The welcome dollars were cashed by the Canadian bank. Everybody waited. On what lawyers call the Appointed Day, the correct proportion of marked adult fish, emerged from the ocean, wagged their tails and returned to their original Canadian habitat. That is the tale. Until we know more about the biology of the spawn, the fry and the extra-matrimonial possibilities of the male smolt, it would appear wiser to expend our cash and our energies in preserving the salmon we have got rather than in artificially controlling birth production.

Because our rivers are the cradle of the salmon and the migratory trout, we might well imagine that we could affect the prosperity of the return to a far greater extent than graphic data has revealed. This assumption only refers to those rivers that have been unmolested by the major dislocations alluded to in Chapters II and III. Providing that there are reasonable opportunities for ascendent fish, suitable redds and fair preservation, there is very little which any Board can do to improve the average annual upward run ; nature holds the ace and king. In most rivers the fry and smolts can find the food they need unless there is unfair competition with coarse fish. Mr. Hutton has pointed out that good spawning years correspond little with the subsequent appropriate return. Every river appears to carry its fixed potential of emigrant smolts, but, according to Dr. A. Huntsman of Canada, this is very much lower than one might expect. The surplus disappears. Thus it would seem that while one may aspire to restore a potential fairly quickly, one is unlikely to amplify it. In a river that has had a fair chance, the propagation of stock can look after itself. Clearly it is the job of the Conservators to assure this fair chance. The idea that if we protected our salmon rivers more we should recover a legendary bygone glory is difficult to prove as we have so few yardsticks by which we may measure the past. I know that Dr. A. Went, who has concerned himself with old records, has found little to suggest a lost Eldorado.

Rod-men may justly complain that they do not get a fair share of the fish that come through, and to that extent glory is departed. Nets are a very poor method of meeting the market. They are unequal in their harvesting and require gross over-manning. The killing hatch needing very few workers, such as that used on the Shannon, has an advantage over the fairest type of netting, although on that river stake-nets lower down the estuary are still worked by the E.S.B. The one-third maximum catch permitted on the Shannon cannot be approximated with ordinary commercial nets. The plan of retarding the net season for a month before the date the rods commence seems reasonable when combined with nights off and a week-end "slap." As worked on the Slaney, we have noted some obvious defects. Fish running in March will not give the upper reaches the stock they need for the season, and the net-men lose the benefit of the more expensive early run. If there is low water in April, fish will move up and down the netted estuary with the tide, and only a few small single runners will get through. This happened in 1946, which gave the netters the best take they had for ten years, but with disastrous consequences to the rod men. It is highly contestable that fish travel any distance at night, and if the estuary is long they cannot make it in daylight. Floods alone can send stock up the river, and they probably work unfairly for the nets, which get torn by the flotsam coming down. Under trap control there is a fixed daily ratio ; the two-thirds of the take can be released throughout the season, be the water high or low. Fish are thus released in parties, encouraging the favourable school habit, which contributes to a better take. For rods to claim that there should be no netting " in order to improve the stock " is foolish indeed. On spring fishing rivers the summer stock may often be the best harvest for the nets, which no one would wish to deny them. If, however, salmon-rod fishing is to be encouraged as a national asset, bringing in more money than the figures gained in the commercial net-take during the spring months, then some fairer apportionment based on a daily ratio will have to be found. Later, where summer-rod fishing is unpractical, a more generous ratio might be allotted to the market. Home salmon is a valuable food, though not one enjoyed at lower income levels.

The expenses of river protection are so high that one regrets the wasted zeal displayed by bailiffs (or keepers, as we must now call them in Ireland). When the season opens they often run up and down the banks inspecting licences, when a letter from the Board to responsible bank owners should avoid this waste of time and whisky. Their other delight is to pounce on some unfortunate who unwittingly gaffs a kelt. Which of us has not—and who could want to ? Bearing in mind that it is illegal to keep a spent fish, and that an angler's own views on the merits of the law will not interest the judge who may be trying him, we may ask what do most anglers think about the value of the kelt ? The opinion is fairly general : the male is almost surely doomed in any case, but the odds against the female's return are not so strong as to admit of her destruction. Anyway, the creatures are poor (though not unwholesome) eating, which may often account for their ceremonial relaunching after capture. A returned " spawn-marked " fish never reacquires a full " condition co-efficient," and rarely attains the weight of corresponding maiden classes. A fish that has stayed a long time in the sea before its first return will also tend to make a long absence before its second return, and this will enable it to make up a good deal of lost weight. A grilse will repeat its short-absence habit before it reappears, generally lighter, for a second spawning.

In a recent lecture on the potential value of the kelt, Dr. Arthur Went gave more precise figures than we can generally hope to quote on this vexed point. He stated that at least 25 per cent. of the females on the Shannon survive to reach fresh waters again ; the take is counted and examined. His reasoning is as sound as it is ingenious, but his argument must be taken as approximate, and as covering a long period. Out of every 100 recorded fish, ascending the river, 7·8 are spawn-marked. As only ·005 of these are males, they may be disregarded and the total taken as it stands for females. Of our 100 recorded fish one-third (33·3) are marketed, and the other two-thirds (66·6) are let through ; 15 per cent. of those let through are caught by rod. This gives 56 fish left alive to spawn. Of this number about 30 will be females and 26 males, the slight excess of hens being due to the fact that practically all the S.M. fish were female. Since we know that of 30 spawning females, 7·8 will reappear in the river, we may accept Dr. Went's estimate of 25 per cent. return to fresh water, and 15 per cent. to the redds. Exact knowledge takes more acquiring than loose thinking, and I fear that Dr. Went has made his case. His conclusion supports a reasonable protection of spent hens, more than I should otherwise have been prepared to admit, but he has shaken the slight right to live for the male kelt, and the still greater nuisance, the red cock. One cannot ignore the loss of smolts and parr that is involved by the presence of descending kelts. We know how eagerly they will snatch at a sprat bait, even if they do not actually eat it. It is surely fair to assume that they are equally ready to dash at a smolt in distress ? In the interest of stock preservation, an arguable case can be made for killing male kelts caught on the rod, if the law could be altered.

Since making these deductions Dr. Went has published a further analysis based on 25,000 salmon examined in twenty-five rivers in Ireland during 1944-45. He found that not only did the different river percentages vary from 0·6 to 15·4, but that the results during the two years also differed considerably. The Shannon S.M. fish have fallen from about 8 per cent. of the total run to only 5 per cent., since the scheme disturbed the balance. The figures examined for these two years did not differentiate between the sexes, but Dr. Went tells me that the male return may be as high as 1 in 20, which survive to spawn a second time ; the female figure is 1 to 4 or 5. Therefore the Irish return roughly corresponds to Mr. Hutton's Wye figures of a 21 per cent. return. Dr. Went declares unequivocally that " the larger members of the stock are invariably maiden."

The conclusion that in normal rivers it matters little what we do, since Nature holds the Ace and King, would be short-sighted. Over a long period it is the player who can take with his Queen who is left the winner on even a salmon river. Such a player will be too astute to let a Knave snatch the tricks he has won. We may take it that the most effective policy is that which justly proportions the take between market and rod—and watches and guards the river constantly. It is a fact, however, that as things now stand, the cost of compensation to buy out the nets for better control would be too vast to be carried out, and could not be done without much bitter resistance. While the price of salmon has a fictitiously high value, there is little hope of reform. As we have suggested before, with improved chilling and Cellophane cuts from America, things may change and prices drop ; then only will the rod-man, to whom value means less than the trophy, come into his own.

Wholesale commercialization of rod fishing in any form must have a detrimental effect on sport. With a decent salmon fetching some £4 and, almost worst still, inordinately large baskets of trout being shipped to cities at equally fantastic prices, it is too tempting for the local expert, be he poacher or legitimate fisher, not to throw up all other work while the take is on and strive for the market alone.

CHAPTER XV

"THE PLUS SIGN"

(II) *Improvements to Stands*

THE dream of every bank holder is to make the most of
what he has. With waters scanty, the need is greater
than ever. The upkeep and improvement of trout streams
have had great attention paid to them. They are smaller
to handle than the flow of most salmon waters, and a couple
of men can do a lot. Excellent books are at the disposal
of those interested and anything I could say would only
be at second-hand. Wire "bolsters," and wire netting
alone are expedients which would be useless on the river
where I work, yet elsewhere these have transformed the
course where the flow suited them. I can understand that
on rivers where the water supply has been depleted it is
better to narrow than to deepen by excavation, to aim first
at recovering pace and current in order to avoid the creation
of mud and sand. Such adjustments need tactful rather
than drastic solutions. The menace of our neighbour's
cress-beds above us leading to a deposit of mud, unnecessary artificial hold-ups to retard the flow, all these and
more, beset the modern bank holder. The greater evils
may be obvious, but the smaller can ruin the carry and
the fishing of a good minor stream. Where weeds have to
be cleared one is attracted by Dr. Mottram's advice to use
the hoe rather than the cutter. Not only does this method
keep the beds and the channels between them more or less
permanent, but it avoids the loss of immature fly life.

The chain of circumstances in the smallest brook has its
parallel in the nursery saga, we may say :

" This is our Jack who moved the stone
That turned the flat from monotone,
And flushed the stream with a rippled flow,
That caused the sand-bank down below,
That grew the weed with snail and shrimp,
And screened the caddis change to nymph.
The nymph that winged the careless fly,
Which lived a day and left the sky,
Its passion spent, and just about
To form the diet for the trout
         —that Jack caught."

Obviously the violence of winter's heavy volume mainly decides the confines of river bounds. Unless one studies an old map, and we need not go back beyond some seventy years, it is difficult to realize how dramatically a normal river's course may be dislocated in the water's urgency to force its easiest passage to the sea. Corrosion here, a swamp recovered there, an island cut off, a new turn formed ; sometimes the change is temporary, at others it is what we call " permanent." But there is nothing permanent about a river. We, on the Slaney, shiver when we read the map and reflect upon the shake of Nature's wrist, which ordered our beloved stream to where it now runs, instead of directing it into the nearby Liffey—to share its doom. Rivers, by their nature, vary enormously. The Wiltshire Avon, beside which I spent my school days, never had a flood. The water level was not only disciplined by a series of lockgates (which worked), controlling the dykes along the meadows, but the fine close soil absorbed and gripped the moisture, which only percolated through, weeks later, to reach the river bed. Rivers in the West of Ireland are subject to spates, even though equalized by huge lake systems ; still the same rainfall will not produce the proportionately high water we experience on the Slaney, and which used to affect the Liffey, before the lake was formed at Poulaphouca. Without sustained rain we drop as quickly as we rise. Like the German governess, we are easily cast down and easily cast up.

Strategic improvement depends upon influences largely beyond human control, but often there is opportunity for private tactics. Coming into possession of a new beat it is not enough to be told of how this or that stand was renowned in the past ; since then circumstances may have arisen, above or below, that will cancel out any effort our piety and wit might devise to restore what has been lost. A mended weir below, a battered one above, may delay or hasten the normal run. A tributary above may have been cleared or deepened, influencing the flood flow, another may now run through extended denudation of turf, undue siltage may have overlaid our submerged rocky floor. The number of changes that are capable of upsetting the character of a short beat in the course of two generations is revolutionary. Rivers that have a gravel source and a shifting gravel floor are so susceptible as to be beyond human aid. Mr. Menzies has given us his experience of the changing Spey, jumping sideways from field to field, and he says that where gravel prevails one can only hope to seek what is good in the new, to compensate for what has been taken in the old. Therefore, in appreciating the situation one has to accept certain prescribed facts, and then study the balance of the stands with an impartial eye.

Let us presume that both banks are under single or co-operative control. The first factor will be the geological framework, determining acidity and rock formation. The less rapid the current the better—normally—is the alkaline content. Rivers tearing down from mountain sources are inclined to spring from granite origins, are floored with granite and quartz, but, unless sweetened by limestone areas, they tend to be acid ; if peat districts intervene the flood water will be still more acid. The bottom on these upper or middle reaches, where the gradient is steep, is not going to be the owner's headache. Every pool will have sheltering boulders ; there will be the solid flat surfaces underneath, so much preferred as a floor by the fish than is a cobbly carpet or a stretch of sand. If there is work to be done, it will probably lie in giving free run to the streams, and in guiding waste water to the centre. Rocks that are exposed at a good fishing level break the course of the flow ; if they cannot be levered into a deeper part, where they will help to form a lie, they are better decapitated. Sometimes the execution can be done by a mason or quarryman, tackling the line of fissure with a cold chisel. If the rock does not yield to this direct attack, I have known of iron cradles made to fit the top and hold a fire. Heat will disintegrate resistence, and the rock's peak can be hammered off. Permission to apply dynamite may seem the easy way out, but the explosion does not always act on the line we should like, and the rock may split and rear up on one side, with a jagged edge threatening.

The results of levering out manageable boulders exposed on a gradient, of freeing the heads of streams, and using the obstacles displaced as holds, has—we find—never failed to do good. The type of work that aims to help both fish and rod is ideal reform, but the fish should take precedence.

Weirs, especially artificial weirs, can be teasers. The angle of their original design (for mill, salmon or eel trap) may be bad for rod fishing. Flood assaults knock them about, or erosion may widen their sides. Never let us welcome a weir as an obstacle put there to hinder the upward passage of fish. Such a policy can only help the poacher. A well-designed weir should form a wide, comfortable stream—preferably well rocked. It should not be steep —a jagged spillway running from a moving glide is the natural model. Without a good gradient no artificial weir will equal a natural one. If the stream created by a weir should happen to end in a deep, quiet stretch, the fisherman will be provided with the best cupboard for storing his fish in readiness for a move up into the stream. Such a cupboard will be worth far more to him than a barrage blocking the upward run and only mitigated by a statutory gap. There is many a weir which meanders diagonally across a stream ; the water dribbles over it, squirting out through

M

holes into an undefined course.   The statutory gap may not feed the central flow and the dissipation of energy results, at most, in a good trout stand below.   It is going to cost money and material to alter such a situation in a big river. We have most of us learnt by now from Mr. T. Rook, and from the late Mr. W. Carter Platts, that the sides of a weir should be at right-angles to the bank—if not a bit up-stream.   They should be low at the sides and submerge as they lengthen, leading the water to the central flow.   Where old mills, head and tail races still exist, one can only study the existing situation and direct the course as best as one can.

Whirlpools and uncomfortable back eddies must be tracked to their source.   Often they are caused by bad shapes or inequality of the stones forming the weir.   Some-times a flood may introduce an undesirable alien in the form of a branch, which may either poke out an unwanted gap, or stick into the crevices and create a bulge.   Some-times a spit of sand will deposit itself and provide a foothold for a growing willow.   In fact, anything may, and does, happen to keep an owner on his toes.   Even on the more rapid sections, it takes only a short length of quiet water for other troubles to arise.   A slowing down of the current may mean sand deposit on shallows ; big stones not con-stantly scoured by running water may create sand-banks. Given a couple of dry summers, weeds will seize on such opportunity and grip it with long tentacles.   The carpet will protect the spit from scour and cause the flow to divide into long channels, bordered by pretty white buttercups.

There is only one cure—to go in and dig the whole lot out.

Deep tails of pools, sluggish in low water, invite other weeds, but, unless one is dependent upon a summer take, it may not be necessary to attack them.   One blessing of a wet summer is the cheap cleaning it will give to a river. Where the field alongside is grazed, the bank's vegetation will be kept down, but if the rotation is arable, then by

June the river's verge is chin high with trouble and casting becomes a feat of circus virtuosity. Only where there is a summer's take will the effort involved repay correction, and usually one had better concentrate on the spots where the terrain is free from transitory loose-strife. The absence of weed growth along the verge is the most characteristic difference between a Connemara stream and one with us.

So far we have been discussing ambulance work of restoration rather than a progressive policy of betterment. Among such, groins or croys are conspicuous. They serve not only to give a dry-foot to the fisher, but also to narrow the stream. Remembering Mr. Rook, let us keep them low and lower still at the tip. The downstream angle forms sand below, the upstream creates it above. Even if one wants to get sand below, start at right-angles and only hook down later. This dog-leg course will fulfil both objects. We had excellent results from two such groins, formed at the inner curve of a bend. So well did the upstream butt build up with sand that it is now turfed and, after three years the stones of the groin are mostly covered. Below the sloping downstream tip a long, tapered sandbank has formed, on which one can stand at low water, while the flow of the current is directed centrally. As a result our inner curve is narrowed and land reclaimed, whereas previously it was eroding year by year. In construction a groin needs to be well sloped—" battered," as architects call it—on both sides ; above to withstand the force of the current, below to resist scour.

Where a projection is needed only to assist the angler then the contrivance of a moored plank on brackets inland and a trestle in the water will avert any complication from flood assaults. The frontispiece photograph shows me teed up on such. The plank is moored by paling wire to the shore. Our most impressive is a double-jointed affair made by Denis. The planks are supported in the middle and at the end on natural rocks, topped by little platforms of concrete which are slotted to hold them. A rise of water will float the planks and swing them ashore. It takes one (fairly hefty) man to poke them back when the river falls. These affairs are carried in for the winter and have stood many seasons ; they bring in a rich return in comfort— and in fish. All our platforms are well tarred and pebbled, or creosoted.

Of other underwater influences the placing of rocks or of concrete blocks have a history either astonishingly success-ful or strangely negative. We have done very little because most of our floor is naturally rocked. What we have done —apart from submerging obtrusive rocks from above— has, so far, been negative. Often, however, it takes some years for improvement to show. Stretches on the Wye and on other level river beds have reacted fabulously to their influence. Nowhere have I heard of disimprovement, but in many places, most assuredly, numbers of conscien-tiously made and placed rocks and blocks have spread their charms in vain. Others have been rapidly submerged by sand. Not having seen them, I cannot presume to suggest a cause. One can only surmise that if a stretch is too near the estuary or too far above it for fish to rest, that no local improvement will delay or attract the run.

On certain bottoms of sand, gravel or small cobbles where boulders are sucked down and partially buried, it is possible that the top portions which are still left exposed may provide the solid foundation which salmon so much prefer to anything shaky. On a long, cobbly flat on our beat, fish invariably haunt the groups of such partially submerged stones that offer a secure tummy-hold, yet these rocks could not provide shadow or anti-current buffers. How often we may see a fish choose a flat stone or slab by the edge of a fast stream and hover over it. Presumably it selects a firm focus, to tip with the ventral fins. For a good type of stand one should look for a wide central flow, falling gradually down a gradient, broken by underwater rocks ; the stream would form its first pool over a firm floor ; after this the run and the flat below would end in a very deep shaded hole, again solidly floored. If quite ideal a flat out-crop of striated rock would bound the western bank, providing deep shelves for shade and shelter. Passers-by might lament that the deep hole below was not good to fish in ; they should remember its influence elsewhere. A beat with such apparently unremunerative cupboards will have something stored to furnish the streams above.

Undoubtedly there are places where artificial rocking may both create eddies for a fly and holds for salmon. There are other spots where some sacks of concrete would pave the shaking shingle. Mr. Platts does not recommend the use of spherical rocks, which he says induce silt formation. Mr. Rook, however, has designed a round concrete model with a sunk iron handle at the top. These appear to be contradictory counsels, but the discord may be resolved, since the round chaps will not remain spherical if they quickly embed themselves in sand. Mr. Marson's idea of concrete pyramids (quoted by Mr. Platts) are what I should adopt if I had to undertake artificial blocking. These are made in hinged shuttering—cleverly half embedded in the ground at the apex end. They measure one yard from corner to corner everywhere ; thus they always fall jammy side up and their shape presents a sharp edge to the stream. (Too sharp, I feel, if one's line were to go round it. A chamfered edge is an improvement.) Were one of them to fall so as to face the current squarely, it would soon be turned into streamline. Smoke tests prove that they form no silt, and they should only submerge very gradually. These blocks fulfil two of our three desires : they give a lodge for a fish ; carefully sited, they help to animate and curl the stream ; but owing to their shape and the fact that they only stand 2 feet 3 inches high, they give little shade from the sun.

Colonel Prioleau, noted for his work on the Easky in Sligo, has recently experimented on a large scale with colonies of such blocks on the Clohamon water, some five miles below us. There the gradient is gradual and there are practically no natural rocks. He has skilfully placed hundreds of these pyramids, working downstream in groups so as to note local results, with the intention not only of forming badly-needed lies, but of influencing too even a flow. He has also employed a number of natural boulders and has formed some croys. Such an extensive operation on a beat, which had dropped in its records from the fine figures of a renowned past, should be an object-lesson to us all. Colonel Prioleau followed out Mr. Platt's idea of rolling the pyramids into the water on ass-cart wheels. Once submerged, they could easily be moved by one man. For the deeper pools and heavier boulders he devised a delightful plan. A raft was formed, supported on four empty bunged barrels. The loaded raft was pushed out and paddled or poled to the site. The bungs on one side of the raft were then pulled out under water; the two barrels filled and settled, when the slope was adequate the boulders were slid down it into the water. Without their weight the two air-filled barrels could readily support the raft, which was poled home! While the new load was made ready, the full barrels were emptied for the repeat journey. Such stage management on one's own water adds immense excitement to the seasons.

I should strongly advise anyone constructing blocks or other work requiring concrete to be careful in their choice of aggregate. The local and convenient river sand may sometimes be appropriate, but not *always*. Concrete made with Slaney or Derry sand will disintegrate within a few years. Any local builder will confirm the truth of this. We ourselves spurned tradition on the Derry and paid the price. I have discussed the riddle with the Building Research Station at Watford, and they tell me that it may be due to too much organic matter often present in river sand; or, they suggest, the presence of an excessive amount of mica may give it low strength and poor wearing quality.

The influence of shade is proverbial. I have even heard the suggestion of making temporary artificial umbrellas by tying faggots together and anchoring them. (I have visions of my trace getting round the cable and of the umbrella making merry on my line.) Our friable banks are so much undercut that fish can find day-time repose, and then move into the open when the sun drops. It is most unwise to cut down bush cover on the western bank. It is not only oygxen that draws fish into the heads of streams in hot, sunny weather. Broken water creates relief from overhead glare. If it were only oxygen urge that takes some of them into the rapids there would not be a fish left in the flats ; whereas we can see that in such weather the flats hide numbers of fish under banks and weeds.

Depth is another factor which sometimes, though not often, may be influenced by man. On one occasion Colonel Prioleau advised a friend to buy a ruin lying near to a very deep pool and to cast the stones and rubble into it. The stretch became a tip-top stand ! The lime rubble no doubt helped in cleaning the bottom, the stones provided lies, but the real snag, the unnatural hollow, was filled in.

Stray lodges may be formed close to the point of a peninsula if a couple of rocks are pushed in downstream of it. A group is always better than a single stone.

Innovators should go slow until they have studied each special problem and the flood influences likely to be resisted. Weeding and many waterworks can fill the unremunerative summer season ; in the winter gates, stiles and banks must be consolidated. Denis does his bank-staking with live willow stakes that take root and hold the gravelly bank. Poplars are excellent for waterworks ; the stakes root and the timber lasts. It is used in Holland for sabots. Unless the run is insignificant it is bad economics to spare trouble. Everything attempted is not going to be equally successful every season or at once. If a well-designed project has not paid dividends, leave it alone, and in time the cumulative preferences may, for no known reason, begin to pay up arrears. Some unresponsive places may produce their happy moment on a year when a good stand slumps. Varied attractions make the nicest fishing. The platinum rule is never to do anything to " better " a really good stand, either directly or by affecting it from above or below.

CHAPTER XVI

SEASONAL SALMON RUNS

IN considering stock betterment we have pondered upon how we may best play the queen in our hand. What are we to make of the two outstanding cards beyond our control which determine our stock of fish ? Which is the ace ? Which the king—the ocean or the river ? Is the stock from the ocean sometimes inadequate for our needs ? For this argument we are taking the ocean as the area of nutrition where the fish feed before the homeward call arrives. Even the outer estuary and its perils may be regarded as local to its own river. It is often argued that in bad salmon years all rivers running into the Atlantic fish poorly, but can it fairly be claimed that this depressing generalization is independent of weather ? Surely droughts and floodings tend to be widespread ? Where they are unequal, as in 1928, the takes from different areas differ accordingly. When weather and ocean collaborate in bounty, as in 1927, then bumper salmon harvests are reaped everywhere. Since both these factors are outside our control, the precedence of ace or king may seem immaterial, yet when a bad cycle sets in everyone tries to seek a scape-goat. Predictions, based upon the supposed influence of sun-spots upon the ocean sources, spring out like measles. If the reactions of these solar disturbances can ever be applied at all accurately to our weather, then we might expect our run of fish to be accordingly disturbed. Until then it would be as optimistic to base our spring bookings ahead from sun-spot to sun-spot as it would be to consult Old Moore's Almanac.

Mr. Arthur Hutton, basing his conclusions on a mass of verified figures, believes that there is no fixed cycle of good or bad returns. The variation is haphazard. He regards the *Ocean* as the dominant factor in the total yearly stock of returning salmon—as our *ace*. River influences, he holds, must take second place, and would therefore rank as our *king*. Dr. Huntsman, who has had special opportunities for observing the return in the long outer estuary of the Bay of Fundy off Canada, tells me that there the flow from the rivers appears to be more influential, and that the ocean supply is less variable. Between these opinions we may be allowed to conjecture that the yearly take on our own river and on our own beat is chiefly decided by the *weather*—the *joker* who will take any trick in the pack.

The sea is responsible for the good or bad proportion of certain classes of fish (small springers, large springers, etc.) during particular seasons, though scale-reading does not support the view that sea growth is better in some years than it is in others. From the river end there have been particular smolt years where, in every age class, the return was good. We do not know whether hereditary or environmental urges persuade the smolts, even before they leave their rivers, to spend a long or a short time in the sea. It is believed nowadays that the environmental forces matter more. That the return tendency is predetermined even before the smolts leave home is largely supported by scale reading. What Dr. Went defines as *Class A* smolts are those who spend an exact number of years in the river, one, two, three or more, but not a fraction over. *Class B* spend an extra few weeks in the river or estuary before they emigrate, and thus before leaving they gain more weight than do Class A. *Class A* have a long sea absence tendency and they make most of the big fish, whereas a high proportion of Class B return as grilse. Moreover, the older Class B's of three and four plus years are still more likely to shorten their stay in the sea.

The present preponderating grilse return in the Shannon is attributed to this smolt B class. Why the change in the river should have created it none of us can presume to explain. Mr. Hutton has suggested that the season following a good grilse run should be succeeded by a year of big springers, while " West Country " believes that small summer fish should also result. How far scale readings from Classes A and B origins support these views we shall have to ask our experts to tell us. The ordinary man still believes in heredity ; the biologist favours environment. Which in the long run will prove the sounder view is a delightful topic for speculation.

During the bad spring years, from 1940 to 1946, in Scottish rivers sportsmen expressed fears that something new and terrible had happened. It was suggested that the drop in sea-fishing off Iceland had added to the enemies of the salmon. Not only were there more attackers, but more formidable rivals for the available food. These theories did not take into account the contradiction that the summer returns in those rivers were not abnormally poor. Why should the ocean factors discriminate between fish returning earlier from those who ran later ? How much simpler to believe that repeated dry springs had retarded the run ?

It is natural for people fishing spring rivers to judge results on the three critical months of their visit. Yet it is more upon the extent of the summer than on the earlier months that the weight of the year's return is measured. " West Country " in an excellent analysis* has supported this view, holding that we have got to expect good and bad years to recur. Certainly, if not in definite " cycles," a change in fortune is inevitable.

It is difficult, almost impossible, to gauge the approximate figure of the run entering any single river unless, as on the Shannon, all fish are trapped and counted. There may be, as we noted in the last chapter, enough flow to attract fish into the tidal end, but if the water is too cold they will not ascend into the fresh water. The same argument applies to kelts : they are not carried down by repeated

* " Salmon Scarcity," *The Field*, December 14th, 1946.

cold floods ; they travel down when prompted by a sufficient flow of warm water. In 1945—a dry spring—the fresh run was estimated at one-third of normal on the Slaney and elsewhere, but even so the rods fared much better than they did with a heavier total run during 1946. This was because local conditions of weather and temperature brought up the fish that were present. In this peculiar muddle the yearly take for rod or net is rarely " average " ; it is either—owing to the whimsicality of the weather—a good deal better or much worse than usual.

Granted that market returns are not an absolute index of events, yet judged on a number of years they give us some guide as to the state of running stock. In Ireland our export figures represent the bulk of our take, and, even during the war years, abnormal home consumption did not affect the total proportion.

Total exports from Eire of salmon and trout for the years 1936 to 1945 and the nine months January, 1946, to September, 1946 :

Period	Quantity cwts.	Our Own Beat. Individual Fish.
1936 - - -	22,570	47 (1 bank only)
1937 - - -	10,518	108
1938 - - -	9,607	42 (1 bank ; bait season)
1939 - - -	12,848	57
1940 - - -	14,849	78 (1 bank until May)
1941 - - -	25,732	102
1942 - - -	21,427	133
1943 - - -	16,926	62 (1 bank)
1944 - - -	11,076	48 (1 bank)
1945 - - -	5,359	179
1946 (9 months)	10,408	144

I owe these figures (export quantities), which have not yet been published, to the courtesy of the Department of Industry and Commerce. The trout export forms an inconsiderable fraction of the totals given. There was nothing in the figures for home consumption during the war to affect the general yearly position of the export.

I give in the third column the humble figures of our own activities to show how very little wider events are reflected nearer home ! It will astonish many people, as it did me, to learn that 1941 had a better commercial take than 1942. This is not supported by the Billingsgate totals, but authorities here believe it to be true of both islands. Our Shannon figures suggest the same conclusion.

Mr. Hutton's figures of boxes of salmon received at Billingsgate, as given to him by Fishmongers' Hall, are :

Period	English and Welsh	Scottish	Irish
1930–39 Average	1,850	11,940	8,055
1940 - - -	1,030	9,145	5,930
1941 - - -	1,059	7,834	9,221
1942 - - -	1,031	6,389	10,314
1943 - - -	245	6,278	9,162
1944 - - -	100	4,866	4,959
1945 - - -	32	2,501	2,192

The average in 1925–34 was for England and Wales - 3,422
Scotland - - - 10,173
Ireland - - - 9,976

(The boxes presumably differ slightly in weight.)

In presenting these figures Mr. Hutton has pressed the point that one market alone cannot offer a fair index. Where Ireland is concerned they do reveal that there has not been a serious drop since 1925 ; indeed, if we take the Irish Billingsgate average from 1906 to 1914 of 7,270, it would suggest that during the past forty years the Irish export is slightly better. An amazing conclusion when one reflects that the Shannon, the Lee, the Barrow and the Suir have all dropped so heavily ; 1945 was generally awful, yet on Slaney the *rods* did not do badly.

Bearing in mind that these later years included the period of the Battle of Britain, of raids, of "D" Day, of countless visiting enthusiasts well versed in the effects of underwater explosives, of fewer legitimate workers and less protection, the British totals bear favourable comparison with those in Ireland. I do not, of course, know how far the many zoning controls may also have affected Billingsgate and favoured other markets, but the Wye figures concur roughly with those of Billingsgate.

We are all used to ups and down in our own lives, yet after two or three poor salmon seasons we are disposed to create bogeys, attributing blame to preventable and unpreventable causes. The good year is, of course, entirely due to our own superb beat and personal skill.

In assessing strategically where the run is likely to rest after reaching fresh water, one wonders how far fish make for and stay where they spawn. In the Shannon the big fellows largely lodge and spawn at Castleconnell, only just above tidal water, where the depth and bottom give ample room for residents. Is this due to the recollection of their early days, or is it derived from the instinct warning them of increasing perils higher up ? On every river there is a distance above the estuary where fish are prone to rest. These places may not record the bumper takes of wider reaches lower down—especially when fish are held up by cold water—but they are not so liable to a complete flop. Then there is the deep pool, so often formed where a tributary joins the main stream ; fish tend to stay there often until August, when they may run up the main river or the tributary. A cold spring should produce fat bags on the lower reaches. To some extent it does so, but it would take more knowledge than most of us can claim to assemble all the contributory or contradictory factors. A flood may be only warm enough to move fish up a certain distance ; then the lower reaches will suffer, the middle prosper and the top be destitute.

So far we have discussed circumstances which appear as the logical outcome of flow and temperature ; what of the unpredictable behaviour ? 1946 had the puculiarity that, despite a generally cold, dry spring, the heavy rains of winter saturated the banks and springs, and kept the water from dropping to the level below which no fish will run. After a flood on March 25th, which obligingly brought us up the stock from down below, the river fell steadily and no break in weather gave us more than a two-inch rise on the gauge until May 25th. There was always just enough flow to tempt up a few small single fish. They sat (about twenty miles above the estuary) in deeper water at the tails of streams. Our usual pet strong streams failed, as there was no quest for oxygen at a temperature rarely 52° F. Possibly these individuals—we did not observe any marked schools—joined the companions they found awaiting them. Anyhow, they sat. It is tempting to believe that the behaviour of an individual salmon may differ from the gregarious one even in the choice of a stand. It has been noticed that even a school of kelts may induce some fresh fish to drift back with them as far as the estuary. Canadian observers confirm that a flood may also take a party of fresh fish down as well as up. On a dry year, when few schools can get through the netted areas, the survivors struggle through one by one. The lone runners will settle down with fish well established, whereas a school would prefer a congenial free lodge to itself. Moreover, the new-comer is less disposed to press through ; he will stay with his companions. A travelling school, while the going remains good, will respond to quite a light rise of water and run on. Such a party may play halma and hop an occupied pool to rest in one above it. This problem of " where they are " adds provoking uncertainty to the ordinary hazards of sport.

If the initial spurt up from the tidal area is checked, and malingering sets in, the best of our stands may remain untenanted and miles of good water may have to wait too long for a later move to save the season. One can understand a general stoppage over a mile or two of water, but how can we account for the ups and downs on individual stands quite close to each other ? We have kept graphic charts showing where every fish has been taken on our water during the last ten years. Only in such a way can the variation in the yearly lies be exposed. It is not enough to say that a winter flood may change the bed of a particular pool. Most of our stands have a permanent rocky character that persists for many years, yet the stock in them will differ haphazardly. The main run may check for weeks at a place where there is no obstruction. In 1946 we caught only five fish on the top half mile of our beat. Our neighbours above us did equally poorly, yet half a mile and a mile below the total hold was normal, some stands fishing very well, others on which we usually rely doing badly. In 1937 an even more marked dead stop appeared lower down on our beat and persisted until mid-May.

On several occasions and after a couple of weeks' drought, with water inordinately low for the time of year, we have had unaccountable pleasant surprises. Fish have suddenly begun a general run, moving up for a couple of hours in water often only a few inches deep. There was no apparent change in weather, nor did rain follow, but all the stands were affected next day. We have noticed this type of event after sunset, but other observers, rising earlier, have seen the same thing happen after dawn. Can this be due to a change in atmospheric pressure ? Occasionally the move has completely emptied a pool that was tenanted before, but more often, like any change, it has meant taking fish where previously there was no hope.

In 1946 fish unexpectedly ran up the Derry (the tributary marking our lower bounds) as early as April, but not to the upper Slaney. Why ? Careful scrutiny of our graphic charts confirm my belief that even the amenity of controlling two banks of a fairly wide river can be bought too dear if it be at the expense of only having a fishing of half the length. On the longer stretch of one bank one risks an uncongenial *vis-à-vis*, but on the shorter two bank stretch there will be less and duller fishing ; some years none at all.

What are known as late rivers have a legitimate run—of a curiously fluctuating nature—that may or may not be connected with what is sometimes called the " Black Run " of January. This run may also occur on earlier rivers that close before the autumn immigration.

Doubt as to whether these very late runners had been hanging on in fresh water or were fresh from the sea appears to have been dispelled by the closely documented Report* on the big accidental take recently examined on the Welsh Dee. There a number of fish, including many normal spring fish and kelts had been killed by pollution in January before fishing legally opened. Besides the usual fresh runners and kelts examined there were present two types of late runners ; some had been only a short time in fresh water and were ripe for immediate spawning, the other type were not so well developed genetically, but were quite fresh from the sea. At that date the normal spawning season was well over. Such extensive material for expert analysing was solely due to the accident, as normally the run would not have been interrupted and examined. During January I have myself repeatedly watched this black type mounting the Derry, and Lord FitzWilliam's head-keeper—a keen trout man and reliable observer—tells me that every year he sees them working late on the redds, on the upper reaches of the Derry, long after the other fish have left. Curiously, those examined in the Dee were all females and it is believed that they may rely for fertilisation on the male parr. Possibly other males may have preceded or will follow them. Whether their progeny repeat the return habit of their mothers, or are affected by other hereditary influences through the males is a further conundrum, for experts. The kelt surplus, consequent on this late immigration, are often a pest on the lower Slaney.

Some such seasonal run appears to have been more frequent at Carysville, in the Co. Cork Blackwater, during

* " Winter Salmon on the Dee," J. M. Jones and G. M. King, *Salmon and Trout Magazine*, May, 1946.

N

the 'sixties than it is to-day, and there is evidence that at that date it continued into February. If, as one suspects, these late intruders injure rather than stock the rivers they ascend, their control may present another problem for conservators. The more unprejudiced observation that sportsmen and bank owners can give to the subject, the more responsible data there will be for our authorities to work upon. For instance, it would astonish me to learn that on the Slaney the late red kelts were more usually female than male. I should have expected the reverse.

Recently we have co-operated with the Department by taking measurements of fish caught ; we record the dates and the sex, and in keeping the necessary scales for Departmental analysis. Speaking generally, the females do (like their coarse fish sisters) appear to run larger. I found it humbling to discover how difficult it is to recognise boy from girl in the fresh small runners, before the male crook on the lower jaw develops. The doctor of our party diagnosed what we believe to be our surest clue. The female gill cover is rounded, but that of the male is slightly pointed behind. Dr. Went, however, assures me that with small fish only gynæcological examination can be relied on.

I am glad that we are not expected to theorize on the data we collect, but it is satisfactory to be able to contribute, even in the smallest measure, to the material upon which others who are better equipped will form a judgment.

CHAPTER XVII

FISHERS AND GARDENS

I AM glad I am a gardener, not only for those estimable qualities described by Lord Bacon, but also because, by looking at a shrubbery one may learn to know whether the stream that borders it is likely to hold fish. During the course of quite a short run the same river may change its nature many times, according to the variation of its bed and of the tributaries feeding it. I had thought I knew something of the Slaney; I had lived on it since 1912 and, twenty miles higher up, I had spent many of my childhood's holidays. Recently I called upon a newcomer, who had rented a house at Aghade, which lies about six miles up-river from us. It is situated just below the rather pernicious acid influence of the Dereen, which enters the Slaney there. The lawn adjoining the house runs down to the river's edge and, as my host came up, I noticed the laden branch of a damson tree bowed over the water. There were no damsons on our tree at home.

" How big do the trout run here ? " I asked as we shook hands.

" I got a two-and-a-half-pounder last evening," he replied.

" Cannibal ? "

" No, on the fly. I've had several good ones." With some pride and before even taking me to meet my hostess, he led me to the larder, where I compared his trout with the mental memory of our herring to mackerel class. Shapely and light coloured, with a small head, this was a beauty. I returned to the garden and was introduced to my hostess. Amicably we discussed the hip-juice which she was about to brew from their opulent crop of *Rugosa* roses. At home we have a hedge of these planted from off-shoots of the same parent *Rugosa*, but we have never picked half a pound of hips. Although the wild dog-rose seems able to produce a family anywhere, the exotic intro-duction needs pampering, or rather its choice of soil. Feeling slightly disgruntled by the comparison between their garden and ours, I sought comfort by remembering where we did better. Our rhododendrons flourish, but another Aghade neighbour, who had previously specialised in rhododendrons, found, to his dismay, after buying the property, that the local soil was incompatible to the type. These two Aghade gardens and the fat trout lying in the larder now made a pattern, with our own smaller fry supplying the contrast in tone. Translated into the revolting jargon of the chemist, they have a local higher pH than we have. Yet had I been asked to mark a spot on the map, where the Slaney might be expected to show the most acid analysis, I should have chosen the situation below where the sour Dereen enters it. Except during flood conditions, the neutralizing effect of quite a small pocket of lime-bearing shale or free calcium will raise the alkaline character of the water to a degree which alters its kind for a plant—or a fish. Even in a flood I doubt that there the acidity is as pronounced as it is with us, but the effect of the favourable pocket is not maintained for long when the flow again runs over a more granite bed, and other tributaries intervene.

The Easky, in co. Sligo, is a small rapidly running river and its volume is largely augmented during floods which wash the turf bogs. The organic nature of its bed varies erratically. During several years, on some miles of its course, Colonel Prioleau took a number of pH readings at different times and places. He discovered that sport at 7·0 pH and over was good, below 6·8 (the standard of normal rain water) rise at the fly ceased, but bait or worm might still get a fish. To be able to gauge one's best chance of a fish on obscure days by a glance at a testing apparatus is highly attractive. To know where the prospects are best, is even more helpful, always assuming that one does not

allow any precise measurement to extinguish the urge to
try out for oneself. It would be Spartan indeed, on rivers
where experience proves that there is a response to such
changes, to refuse a hand-rail to prognosis, since we possess
no natural instinct by which we should be able to " sense "
when our chances are favourable or poor. The appearance
of the water is not enough. Knowingly to allow a party of
half a dozen grown-up people to waste time in belting the
water for a whole day would be conservatism pushed to
imbecility, if the pH has fallen below the local fishing
zero. I would make an exception, and suggest a try at
the earliest stage of the drop, before the toxic influence
had taken hold. Comparator papers provide a rough test.

During 1946 a dry spring was followed by a month of
freshlets, from mid-May. The water looked quite awful,
yet constantly there was a good take. There was a still
filthier looking rise in July, when we had a fruitful two
days. I never remember doing so well during such
apparently foul conditions, despite blank intervals now and
then. When I next met Colonel Prioleau fishing below us
at Clohamon, he told me that while the river normally
stands around 7·2, yet, during those same rather cold,
brown floods, the reading rose to 7·4, and in July touched
7·6. Admittedly at Clohamon the pH should be more
favourable than with us, as the Derry usually is less acid
and the bed of the Slaney changes from granite to mica-
schist. All this confirms the old experience that with two
sources of flow (with us the Slaney and its tributary the
Dereen), the contents of flood water may vary so much as
to alter one's chances. Colour alone is no guide ; sometimes the rainfall will affect one watershed more than it
will another. Such unexpected possibilities give interest and
hope in what is usually a depressing period. Finally, cold
is less favourable to acid pH reactions than is warm
water, and one should note whether the air or the
water is the warmer, and manœuvre one's depth charge
accordingly.

From what we have learnt from the Easky and elsewhere we may reason that if fairly sizeable local pockets can have so much reaction, quite minor changes in the character of the bed should affect a smaller stream. We all know of " spots " that are " taking " for trout, but in a strange river these pet places may not be recognizable. I only wish that there were a wider range of easily distinguished flora, which bloomed or fruited profusely as signals. I have even gone to the length of questioning Dr. Lloyd Praeger, but he could give me no special tit-bit to look for. A wild cherry-tree, I have discovered, will not be scarlet with fruit unless the soil there is alkaline. Imported plants are often sensitive, especially those from Japan (where there is volcanic sub-soil). Whenever I see a clump of really stout bamboos, I know that there is not only material for a schoolboy's rod, but there will also be coarse fish for him to catch in the adjoining ornamental lake. The strawberry tree (*cornus capitata*, once *Benthamia*) is an example of imported plant which only fruits in non-acid soil. Its companion strawberry tree (*arbutus unedus*) is indigenous to the limestone area of the West of Ireland, and shares the same prejudice. Unfortunately, these aristocrats do not adorn the normal streams around us here, and the best we can hope for is to spot a wild plant now and then. Aquatic weeds may be a better guide to those familiar with them. Unfortunately, this is a form of gardening of which I am wholly ignorant.

It is to the credit of the permanent officials of the Fisheries Branch of the Department of Agriculture in Ireland that they have recognised the fundamental importance of the acidity problem. Unless there is understanding of the geological framework of a watershed, it would be unpractical to spend money in trying to improve the fishing by importing stock, or augmenting the feeding. The valuable research work which, since 1929, has been carried out is embodied in six Reports on the surveys. The late Mr. Rowland Southern was the official responsible for planning this investigation, and the quality of his enterprise only adds to the misfortune of his untimely death. "Why," he would ask, "*should* trout be small in acid waters ; why should they prosper, and salmon take, in alkalinity ? "

Two sites on the Liffey were chosen for the experimental work, one at Ballysmutten, in a mountainous granite area (*p*H 5·6) and the other at Straffan, co. Kildare, sited in a flat pastoral district on carboniferous limestone (*p*H 7·8 to 8·0). The reports were based on carefully recorded data, including scale readings, tables of food, mineral analysis, annual measurements, temperature, and weight increments, and on observations of calcium content. Dr. Winifred Frost, my friend of long standing (who worked with Southern until his death, and then alone or with Mr. A. C. Gardiner), was closely associated with all the reports, and the VIth and latest survey*, which we are discussing here, is by her alone. The Ballysmutten and the Straffan trout both ran true to suspected form, although the food supply at the former was ample, if not of quite so high a quality as that at Straffan. For a non-expert the richness and exactitude of the details given may prove embarrassing. It is interesting to learn (here the report is reinforced from English sources) that calcium deficiency is not the depressing factor in acid water that one might have supposed. When water is artificially softened—or hardened—for tap use, the alteration makes no significant difference to a trout's development or to its bone formation. One also learns that the absolute statement about a low *p*H producing a small type of trout has to be modified by substituting the word *always* by *generally*. There exists the anomaly of a lake in Sunderland, with a *p*H of 4·6 to 5·0, where the trout run from 1½ lbs. to 4 lbs. weight. In acid waters the preponderance of carbon dioxide and of

* *Proceedings of the Royal Irish Academy*, August, 1945. Vol. L, Section B., No. 19. *River Liffey Survey VI*, by Winifred E. Frost. Dublin, Hodges & Figgis & Co. London, Williams & Norgate. 1s. 6d.

humic acids vary. Although it is suggested that the former is more injurious, yet we are duly warned not to ignore the humics. Thus the toxic character of an acid flood of a fixed pH may differ according to the sources from which it originates.

In this survey Dr. Frost leans slightly—with all the cautious reluctance of a scientist to plunge—to the side already favoured by Mr. A. C. Gardiner and (far more boldly) by Mr. E. Hewitt, of the U.S.A., that the difference between the growth of trout in a low pH and those in a high one *may* be due to the acidity acting directly upon the fish. Mr. Hewitt goes whole-hog for this belief.* He claims that since the pH of the trout's blood is 7·2, any water with more free hydrogen ions must make the trout's struggle for life harder and put a greater strain on its metabolism. He asserts that, roughly, the pH factor is the best indicator as to a water's suitability for trout. Experience suggests that this is even more so for coarse fish. The friendly stickleback will not endure acid waters, whereas in the alkaline it will so flourish that its myriads will choke up the pipe outlets to reservoirs. This is not to deny the importance of food. Evidence proves that, although the amount of aquatic faunal mosses (on which early nutrition depends) is quite as profuse in acid waters, it has not the quality of the equivalent volume in alkaline waters. The importance of the idea lies in the possibility of an outside factor, acting independently of food. In Dr. Frost's words : " It may be suggested that during the first year the trout is particularly susceptible to the chemical composition of the water, the whole metabolism of the fish being affected by the factor."

If this contention be substantiated it must (I display my unscientific training in daring to use the word *must*) help to account for the depressing effect of acidity, which we have all noted on the salmon. With a fasting fish the

* Recently Mr. Hewitt has abandoned the whole hog for more streaky bacon, and admits the complexity of the problem.

influence, direct or indirect, of food can be ignored. Metabolism may fit the cap. A salmon is much more immediately sensitive to obnoxious acidity than is the trout, which will rise quite well at times when there is no move on a salmon. Frequently a trout will take advantage of the bait we had destined for his betters. None of the evidence produced by the surveys suggest that trout do not feed in a low pH. They eat heartily and are quite healthy ; they breed freely, but they do not put on weight.

The other lesson we laymen may carry away and perhaps later pull out of our fishing-bag is that all fixed pH readings are not necessarily equally toxic. Next season I hope to have my testing outfit, but I do not intend to allow it, or any formal measurement, to go to my head or my heart.

In assessing the setbacks to fishing due to acid conditions, it is easy to confuse this special trouble with the normal upheaval to the bottom produced by any flood, proverbially sickening, or at any rate putting down fish. At such times, too, there is often the extra complication of a low barometer. This will disturb or end sport, after a few days of it, even on a lake. In mud or with sediment, only a minnow or a worm may be looked at, or smelt at ; repletion and sulks follow. One may wonder how much this supposed repletion—this suggested gorging—is actually the cause of the trout's apathy. We know that it, like pH, cannot apply to the fasting salmon. Are we entitled to surmise that their metabolism may also have been affected by prolonged dirty water reacting on their constitution ? If pike and other coarse fish also go on strike after extensive churning up of the bottom, it might reinforce this suspicion, which I only offer in becoming humility and ignorance. The same influence might also account for the paucity of pike and eels in some rivers, which are otherwise akin to their well stocked neighbours. Our bit of the Slaney, for instance, and the Derry both hold pike and eels, but the former has not as many, nor as big ones, as the Derry. If one looks at the flow, the weeds, and the cover, the difference between the rivers is not appreciable. In both there is abundant cannon-fodder in fry and minnows for any buccaneering ménu. Metabolism is such a delightful addition to one's vocabulary that one longs also to apply it to our fellow fishermen. I am sure that Denis's is grand.

Lawyers and scientists share a common caution ; both crouch behind the shelter of the word *suggest*. The lawyer's second defence line is *alleged* : the scientist's *appears to tend*. If the layman, plunging away at effects instead of causes, had always been intimidated by misgivings, much field-work would have been lost. Moreover, Aristotle's old-fashioned natural eggs are like Mrs. Beeton's, coming back into fashion.

I am well aware that pH is not a subject for any amateur. Its quality cannot be measured, even if certain of its factors may produce a pretty colour reaction in a bottle. It is at once a collaboration and a contradiction. Temperature, acting upon water weeds, affects it profoundly. In Chesapeak Bay the variation within twenty-four hours can run from 4·5 to 8·0. Nearer home, in the Itchen, a marked rise has been registered at night. Rainbown trout, always wayward, need a high pH, and do excellently at Blagdon, yet (and how often does *yet* crop up ?) while at a pH of 8·0 they do not need to be barriered, on some Canadian lakes they actually make better growth at a lower pH, where they have to be barriered ! In Lake Pugg (5·8) they grow from 5 to 7 lbs.

Such exceptions do not dismay, they excite the fisherman, who is always faced with exceptions, but they add to the scientist's reticence. Nothing is more baffling than to attempt to extract what he calls " an answer to a leading question " from a scientist. The best plan is first to express a statement which, like the old Scots lady, you cannot very well substantiate. Thus : '' I say, Isn't it queer we never catch them at this or that ? '' To which the expert replies : " Did you fail ten times for ten years ? " I say, " No. I only noticed it this year.'' This brings the rebuke :

" Clearly you do not *know*, (*a*) if a fish were present ; (*b*) if it were a taking fish, (*c*) what was the height, (*d*) the depth, (*e*) the temperature, (*f*) the atmospheric pressure," and so on to (*z*). Of course I don't. Scientifically, my opinion has *no* value ; yet by the constant, unprejudiced observation of coincidences—no less philosophical than the Chinaman's Voluntaryism—is our creel filled.

CHAPTER XVIII

COARSE FISH AND FINE FISHERS

I NEVER can see a float twitch without a thrill running up my spine ; even a cork responding to an eel will excite me as much as it will my nephews or a Boy Scout, who I am supposed to be helping. I know that nothing could be more *déclassé* than to name an eel in the presence of the elect coarse-fish men. Still, there you are ; when the eel excites the old cork to a shiver, pulls it upstream, and then—in urgency—sinks it, I become irresponsibly overwrought. For this reason I, who have had no chance to practice with my betters, have devoured what I could find to read about them. After the economic consequences of the first Peace, it was my privilege to redeem the gear of an expert float-man out of pawn. Afterwards we spent more than an hour while he explained some of the subtleties of the game.

I have therefore nothing to offer those who practise the craft, but I can assure game-fishers that it would repay them to respect it more. As a natural study coarse fish includes a greater number of species and a wider variety of waters than one gets with game fish. Grayling is but a step-child to the trout ; if you can catch the latter, you will catch him, too, although admittedly he is harder to hook. In spite of being a distant and poor relation of the salmon tribe, the grayling keeps no teeth in his smug little mouth. Like those of *la famille* carp, his dentures—or their substitutes—are housed in his throat in the gills, and his mouth lacks the holding quality of the trout. I imagine that the grayling would resent it if classed among the coarse fish, and so, though we have no sympathy with this type of snobbery, but because he has given us so much fun, we will respect his sensibilities and not deal with him here.

To glance at the distribution of coarse fish is to discover a clue to the origins of geography in these islands ; it means also accepting a smattering of geology, on which physical geography is based. We picture the days when the eastern rivers of Britain were tributary to the Rhine and before the land slipped away to establish its own rough island story, distinct from the continental shelf. Ireland had begun its Sinn Fein (*ourselves alone*) existence long before, and Scotland had its breakaway sooner than the southern land block of the rest of Britain.

It is usual to group British inland fishes into two categories : (1) those which have only taken to fresh water comparatively recently and who spend a part of their lives in the sea, and (2) those which reached us long ago, when Britain was part of Western Europe, and which are wholly established in fresh water. Game fish all fall into the first category (even though the bulk of brown trout no longer visit the sea, enough of the species do so to put them in the first class). Several coarse varieties, such as mullets, flounders, eels and the cheerful little three-spined stickleback keep touch with the ocean, but the bulk of what we have called coarse fish have a very long and solely fresh-water ancestry. Of the twenty-two species comprised in the second category all, according to Dr. C. T. Regan,* are found in Yorkshire, nearly all in the Trent, Ouse and in Norfolk, and less and less as one moves westward and northward. Numbers of them are missing west of the Severn ; only ten specimens have reached Ireland, and there are no true indigenous fresh-water fishes in Scotland. We know that Christian abstinence from meat introduced and spread the range of the tench, pike and perch, so, in addition to a study of geography, the student of the coarse fish can claim a word on social history. Not many exotic types appear to flourish in these islands, the exception being

* *The Freshwater Fishes of the British Isles*, C. T. Regan.

the Asiatic carp, introduced many hundreds of years ago. The goldfish variety of carp will live and breed here, but does not maintain the gold standard. Even rainbows are non-paying guests, despite a few successes.

Leaving their context and distribution, and returning to the fish themselves, we will find their names, shapes and characteristics fascinating. Take the bleak, a most shapely little fellow, as the types who fancy strong currents instead of sluggish waters are inclined to be ; he can make himself a pest to serious fishers. The unearned increment of scales that may be used to create the lustre on the artificial pearl is no consolation to the fisher when the creature, sporting in his hundreds, stymies the chance of a worthier catch. Who could resist the name of the pope or ruffe, a cousin of the perch, but residing affluently in the more sluggish parts of the southern counties ? He is, paradoxically, not found in Papal Ireland. He runs small and has none of his relatives' pugnacious qualities, but his dorsal spined fin has a sinking curved line ideally formed for heraldry. The dace, though smaller, is elegant (strong water again) and socially ranks higher than the roach, who constitute the proletariat of fishing society. So much do the latter congregate in vulgar herds that, especially when spawning, you can hear their bodies hiss as they rub together. At such times the he-roach grows a special horny snout with which he prods his females to hurry on the spawning. Mr. J. R. Norman has told about these low fellows, and much more besides, in his delightful book.* I had thought that the flounder always kept his ridiculous profile on the right side of his head only ; Mr. Norman tells us that there are exceptions—the other cheek is in fact sometimes turned. It is baffling to wonder how this could happen, or why ? The bream, the carp (as crafty and intellectual as the mandarins who delighted to rear him), the barbel (looking like a character from Dickens), tench and chub are the standing dishes of the expert coarse fisher. Roach and

* *Fishes of Britain's Rivers and Lakes*, J. R. Norman.

rudd are high on the list, but the pike, perch and bass are special items, not included in the usual competition programme. Before we presume to approach the climax to the sport, a word on the humblest and commonest trophy that can be captured—the tiddler, the joy of every child who has ever learnt to bend a pin. The tiddler—or stickleback—is *ubique*. He is just as happy in the estuary as he is upstream. As a domestic figure the male outbids the peacock, arrayed in a vest of brilliant red he woos and weds, but before he leads his series of adoring brides home, he makes a domed nest of stems and roots of water plants, welded together by his own mucus and a secretion from his kidneys. The ladies are then led inside singly to do their share, and red-breast fertilizes all the eggs. After the weddings the harem withdraws and the eggs are hatched. The father remains on guard and drives off or sacrifices all intruders, using his sword of dorsal triple pins. No wonder that so carefully-sheltered a family has resulted in an embarrassment of progeny.

To the solitary angler even the idea of competition fishing is repugnant ; possibly one might understand its character more readily if one compared its inducements with that of bridge. Bridge may be an excellent game, but no good player would bother to improve his skill unless the achievement were measured by some form of money standard, though not necessarily by high stakes. In bridge it is not enough to win the rubber as one might win a game of chess ; unless the total is gauged by some comparative unit of practical value, there is no valid difference between the scores. Coarse fish, even where the take may be kept, are of little table merit. One is not thanked by the neighbours, and few people have the time or the accessories to follow Isaac's recipes. After pussy, what next ? If there is no advantage in a big bag, there is still less in club waters where only specimens of real interest may be taken. The rest (that is 999 per 1,000) are put back after being weighed. At home there is nothing to show but an entry in a notebook. Not even pussy profits, still less a fish-cake. Could platonic love of sport go further ? Is it not natural that people who have attained the highest competence in hooking and landing fish should feel the urge to pit themselves against their fellows and against time ? Competitions were bound to arise, and it is to the credit of their organizers that they are run so fairly. There can be little doubt that they have improved the quality of the technique, just as high-driven birds have made for better shooting. We will imagine the man who has drawn his peg number in a competition and has three hours with a tiny range of water to get out all he can. He has to shed his ground-bait (the war limitation excluded cereals) and his clouding ; if too little ground-bait is used he may not attract fish ; if too much, the fish present may overlook his special dainty. Likewise with the artificial cloud, it must obscure without obliterating. Above all, whatever he does, he must *not* prick and lose. Always he hears his watch tick on and feels his fellows may be doing better. Fishing with gossamer tackle and the chance of anything up to 8 lb. weight, he needs a delicacy of touch in the strike which fills me with awe. No wonder the " fan " prefers to make his own rod, generally using unferruled cane to allow the slightest vibration to pass beyond the quivering quill float to the sensitive finger-tips. It astonishes me that the long rod, without rings, and mounting the " tight " line of tradition should have persisted until recently for competition work down south. Its use, indeed, is still common for individual fishing. An experienced competition expert must be able to draw upon a fund of lore and of water knowledge ; how many chuck-and-chance-it fly-men could claim one-half the skill ? Which of us is so disinterested in the take as to be entitled to criticize the desire to measure skill and experience with other fanciers ?

I have myself always fished alone, or just within hail of someone else, but then I have had many other opportunities to exercise the club spirit. Most coarse fishers are

THE WITHAM
"Elbow to Elbow"

Lough Corrib and the Free Range

busy men, and how natural for them to connect their
hobby with good fellowship and reunion, especially as only
in co-operation could they even hope for fair dealing in the
best of the crowded waters open to them ? A peg number
in a competition may only extend a few yards, but those
few are the absolute kingdom of the competitor, and he is
facing well-stocked water. He has not got to queue up or
hurry to acquire his right, it is drawn for him. Knowledge
of nature's ways is not found in expanse only. Wind,
currents, depth and eddies can be mastered on a small
scale by those with seeing eyes, weather sense and imagination, Even the size and form of the float and the precise
situation of the leads need minute adjustment.

It gives one an idea of the popularity of such fixtures to
learn that at a recent competition on the Witham in Yorkshire it needed the services of two special trains, numbers
of cars, bicycles and every variety of wheeled traffic to
convey the 1,400 entrants to the *rendez-vous*. Peg numbers
had been drawn in advance and the organization involved,
before and after, included the two hours for weighing the
catches. Here the fish competed for were bream, and the
winner's take of seven weighed 14 lb. It was believed that
his private bet on his chances had brought him in £250.
This element of professional book-making on the river bank
introduces a jarring note. Could not a club " sweep "
supply the " flutter " common to so many sports ? Gamb-
ling is an illogical affair, being to most people a matter of
degree. Cashing-in is however a form of pollution which
can easily tarnish the lustre of fishing, as surely as other
types of it will befoul the water. The menace of cash has
introduced false qualities into the salmon circles ; it could
soon do the same in mass competitions.

Besides the immense field of combined activity, there remain numbers of coarse fishers who delight in more itinerant
moods on lesser stocked beats. Reflective qualities appeal
to them more than do the competitive or even the
associative forms. Despite the bane of over-crowding, the

O

experienced man who works alone can generally find somewhere to go.

The use of the fly (especially fished dry) for chub, roach and dace is rapidly extending, and in the first two instances users tend to catch bigger fish than do the doughboys. I do not claim that theirs is necessarily the higher art, but it is a different one ; the greater variety of methods used, the better. Moreover trout-fishers, deprived of opportunity to use flies for the fish they are used to, can find a chance to develop their casting and technique in striking. Any illusions that they may have held about coarse fish not " playing " will be scattered if they get the chance to hook a barbel or to land a heavy chub among weeds on a light rod, and lighter tackle. A friend who float fishes for chub when he cannot get a chance of a salmon so much respects the former that he uses a special split-cane Leonard rod for the purpose. As for the wily old carp, try getting one of those out in a hurry before presuming to look down on any but " game " fish ! Little carp may take less landing than little trout, but the old carp customers are infinitely more resourceful than the trout. Fishing in still ponds or lakes one needs to be stealthy. One's own—or another's— footstep may create disturbing vibration, more so than would be observed in a stream.

Pike, though coarse enough, hold brevet rank with game fish. Except in strong water, they are the equals of the Indian mahseer ; like them, they make a brave start and craven finish. Perhaps because they are so slippery to gaff, I have not found them too easy to get out. They tend to leer at me with their malevolent eyes and I get scared. What enemies of society they appear, lying aslant even to the stream that holds them ! The dorsal fin of the pike, unlike that of other fish, seems to have slid down the long back, only stopping to form a handle near the caudal fin. The long, naked forepart of the body resembles a serpent. The huge head and gill cover, the mouth carpeted and roofed with armour, the beautiful marking—coated with slime—all combine to make the pike the least congenial of anything that swims in our waters, except perhaps the eel. I find, too, that the amount of ante-mortem whacking required on its hollow pate is a needlessly revolting detail in the capture. But allowing for those prejudices, what sport can one achieve in fishing for him properly! Except for the definite purpose of getting rid of a pest, the use of a live bait is repellant. It may, we are told, amuse rather than hurt the victim (which I do not believe), but it involves as little skill as a night-line. The use of the thread-line for pike and perch in large lakes seems admirable ; its range usefully extends the scope of operations where space could not otherwise be spanned and where the catch can never be too many.

Owing to seasonal variation in spawning, coarse fishing generally extends from June 16th to March 14th. The bream and doughty barbel are the first to recover condition ; as the weather warms up the carp, rudd and tench come into form, until autumn arrives with roach and chub. (The Thames chub makes things as awkward as it can by preferring to breakfast at 4 A.M.) The pike, as we all know, is at his or her best (for the lady far exceeds the jack in size) in winter, but the ideal taking day still remains a gamble. The Queen regnant so far recorded comes from Ireland, where 53 lb. far outclasses the English best of $37\frac{1}{2}$ lb. Over here we believe that fish much bigger still have out-topped the queen pike, but the weights were not officially checked. High weights in the various classes, omitting record sizes which are misleading, would be : bream 9 lb., chub 6, carp 20, perch 4, tench 5, barbel 12, rudd, slightly higher than roach, at 3 to 4. The largest yellow eel taken on a hook was $8\frac{1}{2}$ lb., whereas on the Shannon silver ten-pounders are commonplace.

Female coarse fish nearly all run bigger than the males. Size limits for keeping may therefore react unfavourably on the portly lady perch, as the puny male of the same age is despised, put back, and so lives to escape another day. Old hands of ten years are rarely landed. Until recently the perch concealed their age by resisting scale reading. Now, Paul Prys, with polarized glasses, have taken mean advantage of the tell-tale inscription found inside the gill covers.

Sea-fishing for large fish cannot be grouped as thrifty. Boats and crews cost money, and the catch, by tradition, is the perquisite of the crew. The poor man's opportunity will be from row-boat or pier, and the exploration of this outlet might help to relieve the pressure on inland fisheries. It would be satisfactory if the British Sea Anglers' Society were, after war-time retirement, again to spring into activity, and so influence the development of more exciting ways of fishing off our coasts. In Ireland the " Knights of the Silver hook " (sea fishers) might usefully enlarge their range. While it is comparatively easy to catch the type of small fish that happens to be in season, it seems hardly worth the trouble of making the capture more difficult on purpose. If it could be proved that fishing light with rods mean more or bigger individuals, then we should indeed find our justification. To pull a spoon or a bit of fish skin behind a boat with a light rod instead of a hand-line is not enough. Rod *versus* hand-line, however, might provide an opportunity to introduce friendly competition which would give an " edge " to finer tactics, and perhaps show the way to more attractive execution. At present the line men claim to do better than the rods, excepting in certain estuaries.

Bass, gamest of fish, especially on a fly, are chiefly to be met in estuaries where the stream joins the sea. The bass is the most inexplicable creature in its tastes. The only course is to do what the locals do, as nothing but the bait favoured in each particular port will suit them. The mullet is another tantalizing wretch ; it rushes into rivers in its hundreds, rising and splashing, and it will just take, say, a Silver Dr. often enough to lure one into endless wasted hours. If a reformed B.S.A. Society could guide the new-comer to better methods and friendly openings, the sea, with its tides and currents, might provide an ideal fishing holiday for hundreds more people. As it is the visitor is helplessly at the mercy of the oldest local sea-dog who is willing to take him out. It takes time to master independence, born of knowledge.

There are few opportunities to bend a rod that will fail to fan a latent spark in the enthusiast. I could spend an afternoon watching a small child catch tiddlers, but I am left colder than ice in such a place as Bournemouth. Extended on a deck-chair is an unlovely object with braces, reading the Sunday paper; lower down on the beach is his tripod, on which rests a short, ill-bred cob of a rod. On its tip is fastened a clothes-peg, to which is attached a round bell, suitable for a toy-dog's harness; when it rings . . . I like to picture myself walking haughtily away. I know, of course, I should do no such thing. I should watch it out to the end—and then start asking " braces " questions.

I have not mentioned tunny, because alas ! that aristocrat is far beyond my station and probably that of most of my readers.

CHAPTER XIX

"OVER HERE"

IRELAND (to Englishmen the name *Eire* implies partition from the northern half) can still offer more opportunity for the itinerant sportsman who knows his geography than has been possible in England for the past hundred years. Inconvenient transport in the remoter districts and the presence of less than 4,000,000 inhabitants instead of 40,000,000, partly account for the difference. Yet had our four millions been given a present of England in exchange for this island I doubt that many of us would have fished. I don't know why. In this peculiarity we differ from other Europeans. If my own ancestors had not originated from Buckinghamshire a couple of hundred years ago, it is unlikely that I should have been writing this book. Of the few local people who fish for pleasure nearly all are Anglo- or Scotto-Irish, and even they only fish for salmon or trout. Compare the Thames, the Seine, the Elbe, the Vaal, with the Liffey or the Shannon! The continental rivers are lined with the hopeful of all ages, from the well-off to the poorest working man—but not with women. The psychologists may yet determine the hidden repressions in the hearts of Irishmen and of most women, which deny them this blessed form of escape, so precious to their fellows. Maybe Irishmen and women are too realistic to bother about it, or too religious to need it, or too adult to feel its attractions ; perhaps all three.

How often one fails to notice the obvious, if one has grown up with it lying under one's nose! I only realized before the war that what is elsewhere the most popular form of fishing, was practically unheard of over here. Charles rang me up rather excitedly over the telephone.

An acquaintance from England, representing an important business connection, was coming to stay and wanted to fish. I began to murmur something about offering him a " day " when Charles exclaimed : " Not that sort. He uses a float ! " " Good Lord ! " I replied appropriately. As far as one could be said to do so over the telephone, we gazed at each other. Subsequently we enquired of the leading sporting emporiums of Dublin and Limerick. There was no help or comfort from any of them. Despite these rebuffs, the story, I am glad to say, ended happily. The Englishman did not arrive : he got appendicitis instead.

This experience showed me what I had hitherto missed ; locally we know so little of our potentialities that we could not exploit them, even if we wanted to. We are aware that salmon and trout are valuable assets, but how few of us have appreciated the wider appeal of the float ? Yet game fishing will reach saturation point long before the coarse fishing limit is within sight. As I so often do when I am puzzled, I hurried off to see Dr. Went in his hospitable office in the Fishery Branch. Now Dr. Went is neither an Irishman nor a fisherman, but he knows his job and perhaps because he lacks the two handicaps named, he had, before the war, already got busy. An Association from Manchester were at that time in touch with the appropriate authorities here, with a view to introducing our possibilities to their members. I was also told that the Irish Tourist Board (the strategic end of the Irish Tourist Association) is aware of the position. So far, so (fairly) good. Since the war, unfortunately, the Manchester Association has not been revived and, at the time I write (1947) the coarse fishing liaison between the countries has not been resumed. If this one-time opportunity is ever going to be developed again, it will offer a chance for fellowship between a type of Englishman and his opposite number here, who know each other far too little. The better-to-do constantly cross to our side, but the less well-off (unless of Irish extraction visiting relatives) do not come on sporting holidays. If we

Irish continue to know nothing of what we have ourselves, we shall lack the local experience of value to help the people who may come in the future.

For instance, Englishmen who are not attached to and advised by official associations at home may not realize that the rivers of the south-eastern side of Ireland are, generally speaking, too acid to favour coarse fish—although Co. Kildare and the district around Naas are within an alkaline area and offer good coarse fishing. Even pike are rare in the Counties Wicklow, Galway and Donegal, and are non-existent in Kerry; Galway and Donegal waters are not necessarily acid, so even a geological knowledge might mislead the more intelligent. The Irish Tourist Association are now concerning themselves with such details, and thus giving the help that was previously lacking. Local hotels and guest-houses (working on quite modest lines) would profit by taking trouble to learn what could be offered in the way of coarse fishing in their neighbourhood. Such knowledge is not to be acquired in a hurry, with so few to teach, but those who wish to learn should be told where to go for the information they will then be competent to pass on. At present there is no danger of this great source of entertainment for visitors being overcrowded. Better transport and holidays with pay will tend to introduce more enthusiasts, and such an invasion should be anticipated in time to deal with it, on both sides of the channel. Moreover our incomparable coasts are completely unexploited! In Irish tourism (a horrible word) the increased importance of this form of so-called coarse fishing is likely far to outweigh the improved assets of salmon fishing, especially if it be accompanied by better management. Trout fishing should be able to carry more—though not many more—rods. It is agreed that salmon and trout caught by anglers are worth more than are the corresponding number netted. Coarse fish, which no one in Ireland will eat at all, have a zero export value, and the gain of any caught by rods would be absolute.

Before planning to come here our coarse fish visitors would want to know which ten, of the twenty-two species, we have in Ireland, and more or less where they are to be found.

Fortunately there is an abundance of that great stand-by, the bream, in both the large limestone lakes and rivers. The border counties of Monaghan, Leitrim, and Cavan are conspicuously good, apart from the areas of the Shannon basin. Before the war a few English parties used to stay regularly at and fish from Carrick-on-Shannon. The allis shad, sometimes miscalled sea-bream, are said to run freely up the Shannon ladder, but I understand that these rather rare fish are not considered to be sporting. Anglers used to the run on the Severn may know more of them, and may also tell us whether the barbel, introduced recently into that river, have proved to be a success there.

Tench are newcomers to Ireland and are found in the Shannon and Roscommon lakes, as well as in some rivers. Dace are also importations. Their ancestors are supposed to be survivors from a tin of live bait, which also included roach ; the tin was upset in the Co. Cork Blackwater, where the descendants of the dace flourish ; few of the roach survive and those that do are a nuisance to trout fishers. The unreliable bass is caught freely with a fly off the coasts of Wicklow—Wexford, creditably breaking the blank record for the south-eastern flank of the island, which otherwise is only known for salmon and trout. Bass fishing with the fly is successful off almost all the western seaboard.

The Irish char is more a naturalist's exhibit than a sporting asset, but we have him in several forms. Those who are interested in this fascinating variety of the salmon world should consult Dr. Went's paper*. We have no roach (except the remnant on the Blackwater), but the more attractive cousin rudd is plentiful along miles of canals

* " Freshwater Fish of Ireland; Arthur Went. September issue of *The Salmon and Trout Magaine*, Fishmonger's Hall, London.

and in private and public lakes. Grayling, chub, barbel and carp are nowhere present.

If Papa and Mamma on holiday do not fish themselves, what the U.S.A. films call " Junior " can try for the abundant flounder by sea and estuary. Nowhere can there be more openings for the open row-boat. The big game fish of the sea—congers, halibut, tope and so forth, besides such trifles as sharks—delight in the waters of the south and west, but we have already agreed that their pursuit is beyond the range of the thrifty except, perhaps, in parties.

There remain our two bumper assets, the type appreciated by coarse and game man alike—pike and perch. Recently, in discussing facets of the Shannon Fisheries, I heard complaints : firstly, that a hoped-for salmon had turned out to be *only* a 20-lb. pike ; secondly, that prawns are useless in the summer for salmon, as the perch won't leave them alone. The harvest, surely, is there for those who regard it as such.

All Shannon fishings are under the control of the Electricity Supply Board, with headquarters at Limerick. Only those fishers authorized to take salmon are permitted below the Parteen Villa dam. Above that, however, are some two hundred miles of wide river and three large lakes ; where the visitor may rove at will, only dependent upon the boat he is able to charter. As a child I remember countless happy days on Lough Rea, the central of the three lakes, trolling up from Athlone, and then getting lumps of perch around the many lovely islands. Incidentally, all these lakes give splendid scope for sailing, but only for the experienced, as sudden squalls can rend the peace. The use of auxiliary petrol engines has vastly extended the range of those that have them, and are universal with the May-fly fishers. *Ad lib.* holidays and a boat are not for all but it would be a mistake to think that the Shannon and its lakes can only be enjoyed in that way. Much can be won from the shore. To sportsmen it must be satisfactory to feel that better opportunities for holidays are stressed among the social betterments for which we are all striving. Recreation spent away from familiar surroundings by the less well-to-do will spread friendship between the neighbouring islanders.

For perch, lighter thread-line outfits, with minnow or shrimp for baits give capital fun. Perch are among the best eating and worth-while catching of coarse fish, and Shannon perch often run to two pounds; pounders are platitudes. With local knowledge they, too, can be pursued from the bank, but clearly from a boat more extended sport can be discovered. Perch abound in the shoals of all the limestone lakes.

Pike, many of twenty pounds, and some, indeed, running to over thirty, may be met in any of the favourable parts of the river and lakes. At such centres as Killaloe, Mount Shannon, Athlone, and Carrickshannon, boats and fishermen with local knowledge may be hired. The pike responds to much the same form of temptations that lure the creatures elsewhere. The tradition that the big bait is best for the big fellows has its supporters, and mackerel, herrings, and jack pike are used, mounted with fearsome flights of trebles, and bent to wobble. Many people, however, prefer lighter gear and more happening; plugs, spoons and wag-tail are always good artificials, but, for a slow troll, an eel-tail remains the local favourite. To mount him they remove the head from an eel about 2 inches longer than the bait required; they make a deep slit and run the flight (formed of three strongly-mounted single hooks, in tandem, with the middle one backing the others). The middle hook is stuck upwards into the back; the two others project below the stomach. The gut is sewn up inside, generally with blue silk; bone and flesh is removed from the neck, and the loose skin is turned back and bound round with silk. This makes a firm bait that can be from 4 to 6 inches long. Although pike do not feed upon fresh eels, the tail in action may resemble something else in distress. The question of revolving bait in clear waters is a moot one, but it is likely that rapid revolutions succeed best in currents, in cold conditions, or where it is advisable to attract notice otherwise than by vision alone.

So little has class pike fishing extended to Ireland that boatmen here still believe that all the visitor wants is to be pulled lazily about, while his troll sticks out behind. The West, however, is more awake, and before 1939 ardent invaders were demanding opportunities for greater skill. Persuasive spinners have proved that big ones will succumb almost as freely to a small as to a big bait. Connoisseurs of plugs and spoons select their lures with experienced cunning ; thread-lines and short rods add to the rigour of the fights, but ordinary spinning outfits are also used by those who own them. If the West, in the lakes of Conn, Mask and Corrib, has shown the way, the Shannon boatmen should not be left behind in directing visitors to the pet spots in the right way. Expert trolling along the flanks of submerged weed banks is by no means antedated and demands special local experience.

In some districts cash bounties are given for the capture of pike scaling over a certain weight. Kindly guests are apt to pass on this bonus to their boatmen ; many tales are told of the ingenious additions slipped into the pike to tip the balance, and of the subsequent bewilderment (sometimes even passed on to the local press) at the diet of Irish pike. Under autopsy a monster has been found to contain lead piping, putty, stones, and dry ham sandwiches.

It is natural to enjoy a trophy, even to keep it permanently. In many homes father's trophies have for long been objects of reverence to mother ; but the tiered rows of horns, leering foxes' masks, and floor skins over which one trips, are apt to be regarded as repellent or as junk by the young and arty. Bowing before such storms, father may consent to restrict heads and skins to his own room, but, whatever else he may park there, his Monumental Fish will continue to parade in the public eye.

Such specimens in club, hotel, or museum are apt subjects

for reference, advertisement, or comparison. The wood and plaster facsimile, however conscientiously it follows the original outline and colour scheme, lacks personality ; although it is also less embarrassing in a home. It is easily dusted and cannot break. It needs no special mantelpiece or lighting. It and its fellows (once the habit is formed it always has fellows) can hang unaffectedly over the dining-room door, under the stairs, by the bathroom, above the gong, in fact, anywhere where nothing else will fit. I should love to be able to stuff a fish myself, to understand and reproduce its exact habitat, to choose its shiny eye, and curl its supercilious lip. Well tummied and comfortably sited under its glass case, it represents as much a triumph for the taxidermist as for him who brought it to the bank. I have—alas !—never been asked to stuff a fish, and I have never caught one important enough for someone else to stuff for me. My friend Thomas most assuredly has. Here is the story about it.

STUFFED

My friend Thomas is a somewhat sardonic person and I hesitated before asking him the question that was exercising me. Instead, I sat comfortably silent, my feet on the fender before the log fire, and my gaze fixed upon the centre of the mantelpiece. For an angler I am depressingly temperate and the glass of hot ginger which I held in my hand was only laced with lemon juice. I sipped it and stared harder. Something was queer.

Thomas got up and threw another log on to the fire.

" Well," he said, " what's biting you ? "

" That's new," I pointed to the mantelpiece ; " tell me about it."

He said nothing. I continued : " I never saw a better bit of taxidermy. What did it cost ? "

" I don't know. It was a present."

" Come along, Thomas, let's hear about it."

Thomas poured himself out a draught worthy of a story-teller and told me the following tale :

I have an aunt, at least Eileen has an aunt, and, just after the war, we were expecting her to spend a night here at Dun Laoghaire on her way over from England. She wrote a letter as they all do, entirely about food—our far too delicious food—and of how much she hoped that at least I would catch her a nice fish for her only dinner with us.

" You must try," said my wife.

" My dear girl," said I, " the month is November."

" Aunt Mildred," said my wife, " is English. All the English love pike. They prefer them—stuffed with herbs —to the best salmon or trout."

" Rubbish," said I.

" They do. And pike are in season."

Had I not recently purchased a new five-foot steel rod, a multiple geared reel, and the other enlightened accessories of a thread-line outfit, I might have resisted the plea. As it was, on the early grey morning of the day when we expected the aunt, Eileen and I departed by car for an extremely good little lake, situated about fifty miles from Dublin. (I am pledged to those who discovered it to keep its name secret.)

Eileen does not fish : she knits, she reads, and she assembles the luncheon. Arrived, I pulled out the ridicu-lously miniature rod from the net in the car's roof, put on my thickest coat and made for the lake's shore. Eileen remained in the car, her feet on a hot-water bottle.

To try to describe the initial attempts of the most intelli-gent person, who starts with a thread-line outfit, would entitle one to qualify for a strip cartoon. Father wall-papering, Algie hammering a nail, Auntie finding the needle in the haystack. I was all of them—and more.

By lunch-time I had not tempted a fish, but I had begun to feel touch with my weapon.

" Look ! " I said as Eileen came up.

" Never mind, dear, I'll disentangle it later."

We had our lunch; I was smoking and Eileen was obligingly battling with the over-run when Liam came up. Liam is a man of means, chairman of an important business corporation.

"Don't waste time with that beastly little thing," he said. "There's a nice breeze and the boatman has a can of live bait. You can have his rod."

"No, thank you," said I. "I'm just mastering this contraption."

"But, darling," said Eileen, "I must have a fish for the Aunt—look at all those lovely pike in his bag."

True enough, there were several jack and a couple of six-pounders. "That's nothing," said Liam; "here they run to thirty pounds."

And so, losing caste, I left Eileen still settling the over-run and placed the small rod back in its cover in the net. Compared with it the boatman's 12-footer seemed as gross as an oar. We had each got a couple of small ones when we saw Eileen waving from the shore. She shouted that we must go back; she had to get the butter for dinner—and so forth.

Liam told her to go home in our car; and that he would bring me back in his—with the pike. No, we should not be late, he was pledged to attend an official dinner in town. We fished for another hour, landed a couple of nice ones and Liam topped with a fifteen-pounder. By now the live bait had given out. We pulled to shore; I lay the stiff rod down in the boat with the dead rudd dragging behind . . . and then! . . .

[*Author's note : Thomas took at least half an hour to describe the vicissitudes, his skill, and the resource of the boatman who finally stuck his fingers into the creature's gills.*]

Liam weighed it on his spring-balance while I supported his hand—31½ lbs., and not a gaff mark on its green and

"HE'S GOT AN ENGLISH WIFE"

white striped body. I gave the boatman a pound note and told him he should notch the handle of the old rod. We all had some whisky and felt full of heart as we got into the car.

" Thomas, old boy," said Liam, " you must get that fellow stuffed. I'll send it in to my own man in the morning."

" But Eileen's aunt ? "

" You can save your prospects and cook her my fifteen-pounder. No, I'm not being kind : I don't eat pike. The only person in our house who'll touch the things is the chauffeur : he's got an English wife."

We reached the car and tossed all the gear into the boot behind. We drove back to Dublin. It was a tiresome journey, with a puncture to be mended in the frosty air, but fortunately there was still enough whisky to keep the cold at bay. We dropped Liam at his house in Dublin ; the chauffeur was told to drive me on to Dun Laoghaire and then to return for Liam, who by then would have changed for his dinner.

During this last phase of our journey the chauffeur and I discussed the rival merits of stuffed roast pike with those grilled *au gratin*. Mrs. Chauffeur grilled *au gratin*.

I got out of the car and pressed my surviving ten shilling note into the chauffeur's palm.

" Thanks very much. You might bring the pike inside."

" What pike ? "

" In the boot, behind. The next biggest one is mine."

The chauffeur opened the boot. It was empty. " I'm afraid, sir, I put out all the master's gear and bags in the hall at home."

It was then half-past seven. Aunt Mildred came out of the drawing-room door to meet me.

It was kind of Liam to ring me up ; still kinder of him to insist on atoning for the mistake by getting his special man to stuff my fish for me as a present. He would send his chauffeur in to town with it first thing in the morning.

P

Once again I stared at the mantelpiece.

" A beautiful job ; but, Thomas, old dear, that pike *couldn't* have weighed thirty-one and a half pounds."

" It didn't. It weighed fifteen. The chauffeur's wife grilled the other one *au gratin*."

CHAPTER XX

"OVER HERE"

II

THE first of these chapters, dealing with prospects "over here," was purposely devoted to the least known but most promising of our assets; the second concerns the type of good wine which may be thought to need no bush—our salmon and our trout. Irish salmon rivers are largely privately owned and usually the beats are let out to individual lessees, hence the best chance of getting a rod for a month or more is through a personal introduction, seeing the right advertisement at the right time, or by approaching an agent who really knows our waters. The spring rivers are those entering the sea at the north, east and south, while the great western centres do not usually come into play until June and onwards. There are exceptions, but it is well to know of this rough division. Sea-trout are mostly westerners and are the mainstay of the autumn take on the lakes, some public, others privately held. Some western centres, such as the huge Corrib near Galway, are open; at Waterville in Kerry and at Killarney, or at Recess in Connemara, the hotels control the boats and some rivers and smaller lakes, if not the area. At Ballinahinch in Connemara the fifty beats previously leased to "Ranji" are now under I.T.B. (Irish Tourist Board) control, as well as the fine hotel. Here short-term and day beats for salmon, sea and brown trout can all be had.

Day letting also prevails on the Galway river and at Castleconnell; but for these and many other particulars, including residence, visitors have only to write to the I.T.B. in London, or to Upper O'Connell Street, Dublin. Good as such help may be, a tip from someone who knows the suggested area is obviously better. Those seeking for " rainbows " will discover that only in one small lake (Loch Shure in Co. Donegal) will they stay and propagate. They have been tried elsewhere, but although they appear to thrive, they do not breed.

It might be thought that over here we should be free from the grosser excesses wrought by industry. Our scandals may not equal those of Tyne or Trent, but that is more due to our good luck than to our own forethought. We have allowed effluent from creameries to injure the Suir—try floating a greased line on that once attractive river. The Barrow carries the discharge from the Carlow sugar beet factory, and has also been so much deranged by a major drainage scheme that it—one of the rivers commemorated for its salmon by the sculptor Smith on the Dublin Custom House—has almost ceased to matter for the angler or the netter. Even the good trout fishing has been ruined by the change of flow and depth. The Lee at Cork has suffered from so many grievances that it would take the eloquence of a Cork man to describe them. The added menace of hydro-electricity now threatens it. It would be sad indeed if some solution could not be found even to mitigate the troubles of so renowned a river, or at least to spare its last hours from scandalous illicit depredation. It is believed that our two most important untouched rivers, for both stock and sport, the Moy in Co. Mayo and the Blackwater, Co. Cork, may come under special direction through the application of the permissory powers bestowed on the Fishery Branch by the 1939 Fishery Act. Netting and rods would then be under single direction. On the Moy this position is nearly achieved at the present time by the company which administers much of its basin, but which, of course, is a commercial concern.

The 1939 Act, though less comprehensive than many of us would have liked, has many fundamental qualities, and, we may claim, lessons to offer our neighbours, both over the border and across the sea. Although some of its good provisions were at once enforced, yet, owing to the war and the peace, the most useful were held over by the department concerned, and did not take effect until January 1st, 1948.

The powers conferred by this Fishery Act give extensive opportunities to the Inland Fisheries Branch (which for the present purpose we shall imply when we use the term Department). Fortunately the personnel of the department is such as to inspire genuine confidence, except to the perversely captious. I am sometimes ashamed of the trouble caused to these overworked enthusiasts when they are asked to give or to confirm so much information. Those implicated with like bodies elsewhere will appreciate the conflicting difficulties and " interests " which have to be reconciled or countered. If permanent results are to be won, matters cannot be rushed, or those expecting them will only intensify antagonism and confusion. The best asset is the reputation for fair play ; without it there will not be willing collaboration.

In democracy fair words butter no parsnips ; and in discussing inland fisheries in the parliament of any country the best argument is a food or cash one. What is the professional take worth in food and money ? Could it be increased without spending more money, or much more money ? What is the sporting value worth in food or money ? To burble in Parliament of the use of leisure, of good health, of comradeship will only seem eyewash. All parliaments want to know what we sportsmen can *spend*, or induce others to spend, and how many of us can back our fancy with votes. If this is how our representatives feel about it, can we be astonished if the department, their agent, has to mind its step ?

This preamble is necessary before indicating the legislation under the Act which, being progressive and largely tentative in its application, must owe its prosperity to informed public opinion. Fortunately, the Clauses 35-7, which are to be effective from 1948, are absolute ; there is no provisional or local loophole of escape. Clause 35 runs :

> " It shall not be lawful for any person to use any net for the capture of fish in the freshwater portion of any river or in any lake."

It applies equally to several and to public fisheries and to all forms of capture by weir or trap.   The only exceptions include certain coarse fish and predators, under permission, and for approved scientific and propagation purposes.   Compensation is provided for.   Clearly much depends upon the interpretation of " tidal."   Roughly this will mean water that holds seaweed.   Thus on the Slaney " fresh " will now bar the two top nets previously working on a stretch that was, erroneously, considered as tidal.   The benefits of this restriction are so obvious that its example will create envy beyond our shores, and will affect every river in the country, especially the Suir, Moy and Co. Cork Blackwater.

Clause 36 forbids the possession of nets alongside or near fresh water, except by those nearby holding tidal licences. It is therefore not necessary to be found " taking fish " ; severe penalties are now imposed for owning or housing these engines.

Under Clause 37 the Department has discretionary power, later to control or limit the number of nets in public fisheries in *tidal* waters.   Thus it is hoped that a progressive policy will arise concerned solely with stock development and general betterment.   Anglers are not so foolish or so selfish as to clamour for the abolition of netting—or its equivalent ; they hold that at present the extent of commercial netting is rarely commensurate with a sound and disinterested river policy.

Further future powers envisaged under Part V have even wider discriminatory possibilities ; therefore they can do much good, or be a danger.   Power must mean one or the other. The clauses cover power of transfer of certain fisheries to the Minister, and provisions in relation to fisheries or to lands so transferred. " Certain " fisheries include virtually all such in Eire. We are here less concerned with the many clauses covering compensation, nets, weirs, traps, and so forth, vital as their control must be, as we are with the safeguarding of existing angling rights, where powers of transfer are undertaken.

Clause 64 provides that the owner of angling rights (on fisheries to be transferred) may, before the transitory period expires, apply to have his rights reserved after the fishery is vested in the Minister. It is assumed that all reasonable claims, based on the paying of rates, will be accepted, and that dispossession need not be feared.

Part VI defines the Minister's powers and limitations in the control of such vested fisheries, where boards of conservators will still operate, but upon which the Minister (the Department) will be amply represented.

From this brief survey, extracted painfully from the legal phraseology, it can be seen that our Irish Fishery Act conveys vast powers and responsibilities. The clauses legally operating since its enactment include licensing of vendors, definition and control of pollution, protection against poison, explosives and so forth, but unfortunately the Act does not include adequate police or other machinery to enforce these excellent provisions. Without such power the Act will end with the printed word.

The institution of trout licences (5s. for general use and 6d. for juveniles) and representation of trout interests on boards of conservators is included, but has not yet been enforced ; nor has any date been fixed for it.

It is, however, in the great potential strength that outside interest will concentrate. Probably the " vesting " will be individual and slow. What rivers will be " vested," and how soon ? The Shannon has set an example. What of the Moy, with its abundant and valuable stock of both early and late running fish ? What of the Co. Cork

Blackwater? Then those fine rivers Suir and Barrow, which of late years have deteriorated so sadly by over-netting, pollution and drainage? Could they still be restored if tackled under single management? The Lee, at Cork, is, we fear, already under death sentence in the electric chair. Without protection no model control, however, efficient, will be able to ensure that the harvest won on any river will go to those who earned it. The prosperity of all these excellent intentions centres upon this danger-point.

Anglers are naturally apprehensive mortals. In the exploitation of fishing markets their catches—defaced by gaff-marks—are not impressive; their sport is associated in the public mind with " class " and privilege. Once, however, rivers cease to be battlegrounds for competitive markets, the economic value of reasonable sporting over purely commercial catches will be revealed. Money will speak. No Minister of Lands and Fisheries, of Commerce, of Justice or of Finance will find he can afford to sacrifice assets of essential significance to his own and to all Departments. The extent of the salmon actually consumed locally is negligible in Ireland.

Already the Department has two areas under its direct influence—the Shannon and the Blackwater in County Kerry. Although the Electricity Supply Board has been given extensive powers in the management of the Shannon, it works under departmental veto. For instance, the figure of fish allowed to be captured each year at the Thomond Weir is fixed in Dublin, not at Limerick. The Department makes good use of its opportunity for carrying out scale-reading and other examination of data for research. We have already noticed the past work of Rowland Southern and Winifred Frost and the present activities of Dr. Arthur Went. Best of all is its active co-operation with responsible outside workers in the two Irish Universities, the Royal Dublin Society and the Royal Irish Academy. Anybody living outside Ireland who wants documented information upon what is happening here need only write to the Fishery

Branch at 4, Kildare Place, Dublin, to be told of the many publications and where to obtain them.

The provision to licence trout-fishers should help to control abuses, especially in the taking of immature fish. All parr will pounce with indecent zeal at anything offered, but in April the excited smolt population indulges in mass suicide. In the lower reaches of salmon rivers a strong case could be made for the prohibition of all trout-fishing during that month. If this is thought to be too drastic, then some alternative form of genuine protection should be enforced.

Well-run local fishing associations are of real service both to individuals and to the sport, and should prevent over-crowding and irresponsibility. The Dublin Trout Anglers' Association holds a high place among such bodies, therefore their recommendations on fishing control, circulated among kindred bodies, must receive respectful attention. It suggests the appointment of an Honorary Board of Directors, with ex-officio members of responsible bodies and repre-sentatives of the trout licencees. The Board should be empowered to hold and to control fisheries. The waters to be acquired by them should include all unrated waters and those now administered by the E.S.B. and the Land Commission. The Board would assist in the development of fisheries and in the encouragement of research. There would be local administration, and provisions made for finance, largely based on optimistic hopes of a " grant."

I have only seen the report of the circular referred to in the preceding paragraph, as given in *Irish Angling*, Sep-tember to October, 1946, therefore I may have missed a more explanatory account. As it stands there, one notes a fatal omission. This is not a case of the baby being thrown out with the bath-water, the nurse has forgotten to put him into the bath at all. Powers of better protection and still more protection are fundamental to any scheme for improvement. The word " protection " is not named in the record given. The stock now available would prob-ably be doubled if what we have got were adequately

protected.   Take Killarney, where the lake fishing has fallen
off so seriously.   Previously the streams feeding and draining the lakes were under private ownership and were really
well preserved.   Salmon survived to run into the lakes
and trout could safely mount the incoming streams for
spawning.   All the fancy notions for betterment avail
nothing beside these losses.   Taking the waters which it
is suggested should be held by the Board, I do not feel
competent to discuss whether the E.S.B. or the Land Commission should hold or lose control, but the airy proposal
to acquire all " unrated " fishings, without by your leave
from or without compensation to, the dispossessed owners,
is confiscation.   Those who control trout-fishing on a river
running through their pleasure-grounds pay no fishing rates
because one has never been struck ; neither do they pay
rates on their tennis courts as such.   To permit strangers
to meander over people's property and use their gates at
will and share their sporting amenities would be an in-
tolerable intrusion.   Many people controlling small rivers
have paying guests, so the loss would injure, not improve,
the tourist outlook.   Owners of trout waters, rich and poor,
have extended wide hospitality to visitors, especially to
their own local neighbours and associations.   It would be
another matter if long-distance strangers were to claim
such privilege as a right and spoil the owner's own sport.
What inducement would this give him for clearing branches
and weeds and often in stocking ?   Were this vesting to be
carried out on an " appointed date," all the private preservation would vanish overnight and the troubles of Killarney
would be duplicated all over the country.   Development
and preservation of all worthwhile fishing is expensive ;
the cost is only lowered when there is willing local co-
operation.   To attempt to establish it on what would be
deep-seated resentment would double the cost and halve
the output.   I give these comments because the whole
position reflects some of the troubles and difficulties of
attempting to provide equal opportunities to all people.

The Dublin trout-men's report largely shows the genuine
desire for improvement in the undeveloped areas where
the trout run smaller and are less " in the news." There
are also rivers with not many takeable trout, but where,
if weeds could be dealt with, there would be some compensation in the hope of a pike. Game and coarse interests
could and should keep in touch. There are more than a
few places with an odd chance of a salmon during special
favourable conditions. Here it would be most unreasonable
to insist on the possession of a full salmon licence. Where
there is a local association in the neighbourhood it should
be entitled to impose a local exemption bye-law. If none
were made everyone would gladly co-operate in shielding
a technical offender.

The I.T.A. grades hotels in its official lists according to
services provided and the standard maintained ; it would
not be simple to assess fishing standards so precisely since
they vary with the seasons and according to the whims of
nature. The association would, however, be justified in
guarding visitors against over-crowding of rods and misleading information. Speedy profits mean slow returns of
those exploited. If matters are left solely to the forces of
supply and demand, to-morrow will be asked to pay for
to-day. Guidance as to where fishing is free or available in
the more remote districts is needed. There are enterprising people with small cars and still smaller folding
boats who would willingly adventure on the many minor
lakes of the west if they knew where they were permitted
to do so. Such facilities, if known in advance, would add
attractive variety and independence to a holiday. Organization intelligently decentralized ought not to mean red
tape, but red-letter holidays for more people. Our fishing
tackle firms in Dublin, Cork, Limerick, Galway and elsewhere would act as excellent agents to the traveller. To
recommend them would be no more a trade advertisement
than to recommend a hotel.

Ireland is renowned for her 100,000 welcomes ; would

that she could extend this number to game-fishers ! Only wishful thinkers, with tills to be filled, pretend to believe that she can do so. Nothing could be more fatal than the attempt to overstrain the attack upon our stock, even though our actual waters do not appear to be scant. This danger, where coarse fish are concerned, should not arise for many years to come, but the margin of surplus for game fish is not substantial, although very much could and should be done to extend the chances of sport. No Englishman can blame sportsmen here for not wishing to pawn their birthright in the manner of Omar's vintner who sold goods more precious than he could buy. What local rod-fishers justifiably fear is exploitation on the part of hotel-keepers and others of what used to be enjoyed by residents and may now, through injudicious over-crowding, be lost to everyone. This, like so many other world problems, is a matter of degree, which is not to say that it is easy of solution. Industrialized tourism can quickly defeat itself for the type of visitor we should most like to attract. Our natural beauties and our natural sport are assets that mean more than ever to our neighbours who are jaded with substitutes. Yet were we to cash in and over-popularize— i.e. vulgarize—these assets we should find we had nothing left but the substitutes which our visitors had left behind at home.

Fortunately there are clear targets for immediate and future betterment ; we should aim first to develop all that is possible and then, with the help of the many visiting friends that we have made, decide where the danger-line should be drawn both for ourselves at home and for our guests who have learnt to value our attractions.

INDEX

(Place and river names not included.)